D1037336

I've travelled the world twice over,
Met the famous: saints and sinners,
Poets and artists, kings and queens,
Old stars and hopeful beginners,
I've been where no-one's been before,
Learned secrets from writers and cooks
All with one library ticket
To the wonderful world of books.

© Janice James.

The wisdom of the ages
Is there for you and me,
The wisdom of the ages,
In your local library.

There's large print books
And talking books,
For those who cannot see,
The wisdom of the ages,
It's fantastic, and it's free.

Written by Sam Wood, aged 92

PIERRE LALANDE:
SPECIAL AGENT

In 1940, Dutchman Guido Zembsch-Schreve joined his country's army-in-exile in Canada, returned to England, joined the SOE, was parachuted into France, where he ran a highly successful resistance network, dropped his guard for a moment and was arrested by the Germans. What happened to him thereafter is so horrifying that it is virtually impossible for ordinary mortals to understand how he survived. To come out of one concentration camp was improbable enough. To survive two, and a slave labour camp, seems incredible. Here, with modest humour and total lack of bitterness, he tells his story.

GUIDO ZEMBSCH-SCHREVE

◆

PIERRE LALANDE:
SPECIAL AGENT

The Wartime Memoirs of
GUIDO ZEMBSCH-SCHREVE

with an Introduction by
M.R.D. FOOT

translated by
JOHN BROWNJOHN

Complete and Unabridged

ULVERSCROFT
Leicester

First published in Great Britain in 1996 by
Leo Cooper
Barnsley, South Yorkshire

First Large Print Edition
published 1998
by arrangement with
Pen & Sword Books Limited, London

British Library CIP Data

Zembsch-Schreve, Guido
    Pierre Lalande: special agent—Large print ed.—
Ulverscroft large print series: non-fiction
    1. Zembsch-Schreve, Guido
    2. World War, *1939 – 1945*—Personal narratives,
Dutch 3. World War, *1939 – 1945*
—Prisoners and prisons, German
    4. World War, *1939 – 1945*—Underground movements
    5. Large type books
    I. Title
    940.5′481′492

    ISBN 0–7089–3888–4

Published by
F. A. Thorpe (Publishing) Ltd.
Anstey, Leicestershire

Set by Words & Graphics Ltd.
Anstey, Leicestershire
Printed and bound in Great Britain by
T. J. International Ltd., Padstow, Cornwall

This book is printed on acid-free paper

TO
JACQUELINE

Introduction

This is a war story with a difference: a tremendous tale of courage, tenacity and survival, modestly told; and every word of it true.

Guido Zembsch-Schreve was born in Switzerland in 1916, the youngest child of a Dutch neurologist; brought up to speak several languages fluently, and to think before he spoke. Slight in build, he is bright in brain, and able to shift his personality rapidly to suit the company he finds himself in; rare gifts for the secret agent he became.

When in May, 1940, world war suddenly overran the Low Countries, he was a shipping clerk in Antwerp. He got away by motor car, using his own strong initiative, across Belgium, past Paris, down to friends on the French Riviera and so to the Pyrenees; cast up, through Portugal, in Canada; and instead of taking any of the chances of a quiet life that offered, joined the Dutch army in exile as a private.

This seemed tame to him and when he found himself part of the Princess Irene Brigade near Wolverhampton he volunteered for the commandos. He went through, and here vividly describes, the full rigours of commando training and took part — one of a landing party of two — in a small raid on Sark, which secured a prisoner. He was versatile enough to conduct the prisoner's first interrogation on the boat back across the Channel.

He was next picked out by the Special Operations Executive, the subversive branch of the then inadmissible secret service, and embarked on more serious training in clandestine life. He met SOE's mainspring, General Gubbins, and got his detailed training from the meticulous Leslie Humphreys, who ran the escape section. He solved quite neatly the problem put him for his final security test — to establish whether a woman in Liverpool was reliable or not — by becoming her lover before she was arrested.

After what he had been through already, parachute training presented no problems: he was back in France, by parachute, with a wireless operator, late in the summer of 1943. His account of their mission provides a splendid set of examples of when it is worth following the rules strictly, and when one can simply rely on common sense. Common sense and good luck combined, over and over again, to pull him through troubles as he tackled a dual task. He had to set up an escape line for agents, ideally to run from Delfzyl on the north Dutch coast right through into Spain; and he had to arrange for a shorter goods line to move stores (badly needed, he understood, by the RAF) from Geneva to Barcelona. Pierre Lalande was one of his many cover names; he must often have had trouble remembering who, at any given moment, he was.

After seven more and more hectic months, he made a slip. He went to a bar rendezvous in Paris himself, instead of sending a stooge; the Germans picked him up. They neither identified nor tried him, but they tortured him, repeatedly, and in the end packed him off to Buchenwald concentration camp, from which he was moved on to the still more fearsome Dora. Dora was a slave labour camp in the Harz mountains, from which the labourers were told on arrival that the only way out was through the crematorium chimney. Their task was to make V2 rockets; they managed it so badly that over half the rockets Dora turned out malfunctioned. Not even Auschwitz can have been any nearer hell on earth.

Even Dora Zembsch-Schreve managed to survive; he even, in the war's closing convulsions, managed to escape from one of the columns in which the SS tried to shepherd their captives across north-west Germany. By a typical gesture, General Gubbins himself met his plane when at last he returned to England to be debriefed. Close to the centenary of the General's birth, just past its author's own eightieth birthday, this book by one of SOE's outstanding agents makes a fitting tribute to that still undervalued service and records for later generations what devotion to freedom really means.

M.R.D. Foot

Prelude

MY father was over fifty when I first saw the light at Berne in 1916. Formerly medical director of the hospitals of Rotterdam, he had by then retired to Switzerland for health reasons after a professional career spanning thirty years.

I always cherished the greatest respect for both my parents: the masterful father who ruled us with a rod of iron and the softhearted, affectionate mother who reared me, together with my elder sister and brother, in a warm and loving family atmosphere. We children formed a close-knit trio of which I was undoubtedly the most restless and mischievous member.

Some of my earliest and most vivid memories are of the holidays we spent together in the Swiss Alps, and of 1921 in particular. That was when, as a boy of five, I made the acquaintance of a honeymoon couple whose marriage was blessed five years later with the birth

1

of a daughter. It is to her, who was to become my wife, that I dedicate this book.

Although officially retired, my father had to visit Holland so often, where he was much in demand as a consultant, that in 1923 he decided to move to neighbouring Brussels. It was in Belgium, therefore, that I received my primary and secondary education, though the many trips we children made throughout Europe in our father's company were a broadening experience made still more so by his daily doses of general knowledge. This, coupled with my early years in polyglot Switzerland, steeped me from the outset in an environment whose multilingualism was to prove extremely useful to me later on.

As a neurologist, my father took a special interest in the subject of institutions for the mentally sick. When National Socialism reared its head in the 1930s he was quick to perceive the dangers inherent in that ideology. His diagnosis after listening to Hitler's tirades on the wireless was unequivocal: 'The man's insane!'

Although his attitude was not fundamentally anti-German, being coloured by his time as a student at Heidelberg, he was only too familiar with the German ethos and felt — rightly so, as it turned out — that the world was in dire peril. He was also aware of the similarities existing between Stalinist Communism and the methods employed by up-and-coming National Socialism. The sage advice he gave me — never engage in any form of dishonest compromise, always appreciate the worth of the individual human being — is still ingrained in me to this day.

Another piece of paternal advice: Get to know the world and its varied inhabitants. At sixteen, having completed my secondary education, I was sent by my father first to England and then to the United States, where I worked part-time in the offices of the Holland America Line and attended courses at the Harvard Business School, acquiring the practical experience of life which no amount of schooling can ever impart. At nights I washed innumerable cars to earn the few dollars that would enable me to go out on the town with my friends. It was a hard lesson, after the pampered life I had always led at home, but it certainly taught me the value of money.

Meanwhile the storm clouds that were gathering over Europe cast a shadow across our family as well. In 1936 my sister had married an Austrian army officer. Two years later, when Hitler annexed Austria and transformed it into a German fiefdom, the fact that my brother-in-law was related to the Hapsburgs rendered him suspect in the eyes of the Nazi authorities. He was arrested, imprisoned and expelled from the Army. Like his godfather, Archduke Joseph Ferdinand, who had been incarcerated at Dachau, he was released at the instigation of the Vatican but compelled to move with his family to Steyr, where he lived under surveillance and worked in a factory.

By August, 1939, I was living in Philadelphia as a full-time employee of the Holland America Line. This shipping company, which had bought the old German Red Star Line, was having problems in Antwerp because of the growing number of Jews who had obtained visas for the United States and were waiting to depart. Transferred there by the company to help cope with this influx, I sailed for Europe in the SS *Statendam* and reached Southampton on the day war broke out.

The usual Le Havre run had been suspended, so we made our way to Rotterdam through the minefields that had already been laid in the Channel and North Sea with all our lights blazing and the ship's sides bearing 'HOLLAND' in big white letters to denote that she sailed under the flag of a country that was still neutral.

Having visited my parents in Brussels, I took up my duties at the Holland America agency in Antwerp.

Few people realized at that stage what the war signified. Poland and Czechoslovakia were merely names on a map, the Maginot Line seemed to render French territory proof against invasion, and it was assumed that the neutrality of Holland and Belgium would be respected.

Such, at least, were the cosy illusions

cherished to their cost by our politicians and generals. They would have done better to read and heed the book on *blitzkrieg* tactics written by a young French army captain named Charles de Gaulle.

1

Blitzkrieg — May 1940

I HAD found myself a comfortable apartment on the first floor of an old family mansion in one of Antwerp's handsome suburbs. The war seemed very remote, the front was static and everyone had settled down to enjoy a happy, carefree summer. But then came 10 May, 1940.

Just before 5 am I was awakened by an infernal din and a fiery glow in the sky, so intense that it penetrated my bedroom curtains. The blackbirds that always sang in the garden outside my window had fallen silent. I was overcome by a sense of foreboding.

The aerodrome at Deurne and the Gevaert film laboratories were less than a kilometre away and the bombs destined for those targets shook the old house to its foundations. The big bay window leading to the garden blew in and disintegrated.

Interspersing his news flashes with the strains of the *Brabançonne*, the Belgian national anthem, a radio announcer informed us that Holland had been invaded by German troops. Rotterdam had already been reduced to rubble and Belgian frontier fortresses were under enemy fire. The war had caught up with us at last.

I got dressed in a hurry and drove off, but not before taking the precaution of stowing a few clothes and essentials in my car. A ship was scheduled to sail for the States that day, so I had to get to the office urgently and take stock of the situation.

By six o'clock I was outside the office building in the Place du Meir. It was a chaotic scene. Hundreds of Jewish refugees desperate to catch the next boat, were jostling to be first in line. We would obviously have to keep the doors closed and admit the panic-stricken people one at a time. The crush was so great that the big office windows were in danger of caving in under the pressure.

Together with a Yiddish-speaking colleague, who had just turned up, I

8

threaded my way through the vociferous crowd and managed to reach the rear entrance, which was situated in a side street. Then, from a first-floor window, we harangued the crowd and made them a promise we knew we couldn't keep: they would all get a berth on the next boat as soon as order was restored and we could complete the formalities in peace. Thanks to the arrival of two rabbis and the representatives of various Jewish organizations, our plea was heeded.

Having managed to reach the company's Rotterdam headquarters by phone, we were instructed to hasten the departure of the *Penland*, the ship currently in port. We were further instructed to man the office round the clock and act at our own discretion.

The *Penland* sailed that evening.

How many passengers were on board? Two thousand, possibly more — we would never know for sure. It was the purser's job to find some means of feeding and accommodating them. We watched the ship steam slowly out into the Scheldt estuary at sunset, laden with perhaps three times her authorized number of passengers. Unluckily for those Jews who had been left behind on the quayside, there would be no more sailings. Many of them were destined to die in German or Polish concentration camps.

Our only remaining task was to issue priority tickets for hypothetical sailings from Le Havre or Cherbourg. The prospective passengers who bought them would have to get there under their own steam.

In spite of everything, we continued to hope for the best. French and British troops were moving into Belgium and would doubtless manage to stem the enemy invasion, as they had in 1914.

Our hopes were soon dashed by the news that German armoured formations had breached the French line at Sedan. The bulk of the army opposing them consisted of men who hailed from the 'Red' suburbs of Paris, and at this juncture Russia was Germany's ally. Infiltrated by communist agitators, they offered no more than token resistance. If only they could have glimpsed the future, those of them who later joined the Resistance and acquitted themselves bravely in the ranks of the FTP, the communist-dominated *Francs-Tireurs et Partisans*!

The Belgian fortifications in the Liège area and on the Albert Canal were overwhelmed and the enemy poured through the resulting gaps in the Allied line. The British and French armies retreated, abandoning most of their equipment. Resistance in Holland was only sporadic. The Dutch commander-in-chief, General Winkelman, surrendered rather than see his country totally devastated. Queen Wilhelmina, together with her family and government, took refuge in England to plan the liberation of our country in concert with the authorities in Holland's overseas possessions.

With the Germans now only twenty kilometres from Antwerp, it was decided to close our office. We were given the choice between staying and leaving, and the office safe was raided in order to pay any arrears of salary owed to those who opted for departure, myself included.

I had brought a treasured possession with me on leaving the United States a few months earlier — a Chevrolet coupé.

Having acquired a small trailer from an Antwerp scrap merchant, I loaded it with anything I thought might come in handy. I also took the office records and any remaining cash for delivery to the company's office in Paris. By courtesy of some British troops who were destroying stocks of petrol as they withdrew, I obtained a sufficient quantity in cans to take me a thousand kilometres or more.

I paid a flying visit to the family home in Brussels, just long enough to bid my parents *au revoir* and receive a few words of advice and encouragement from my father. Not that I could have known, five eventful years were to elapse before our next reunion.

The lilac was in blossom in the garden, I remember. It was 16 May, 1940.

* * *

And so, with car and trailer filled to capacity, I set off on the long drive to Paris. The main roads to the south were choked with troops whose movements made little sense. Some were hurriedly

12

retreating in apparent disorder, others advancing north and east. Trusting to my watch and the position of the sun as aids to navigation, I followed the minor roads instead.

Despite the glorious weather, a peculiar atmosphere reigned in the countryside. The farmers who would normally have been at work in their fields had disappeared, but the landscape was far from deserted. Long columns of refugees fleeing from the advancing Germans stretched away to the horizon, their multifarious means of transport piled high with furniture, mattresses, even pigs and chickens. I saw one old man driving a small herd of cows — where to, God alone knew. Fear had left its mark on every face. Memories of the First World War and its ordeals were all too fresh.

Early on 17 May, my twenty-fourth birthday, I reached the vicinity of Noyon, less than a hundred kilometres north-east of Paris. It was a warm, sunny morning and I stopped for a refreshing wash in the crystal-clear water of a little stream. Nothing could have seemed more idyllically peaceful than that rural scene.

Soon afterwards I joined the main road that would take me to Paris. An artillery unit rumbled past, heading for the front, the men's set faces filled with grim determination. And then I heard the drone of approaching aircraft.

It was mid-morning by now. The long, straight road leading to the water-tower on the outskirts of Noyon was flanked on the left by a small wood and a sizeable ditch.

The drone of engines swelled to a roar, and before I knew it bombs were raining down on the little town ahead of us. These sudden detonations were succeeded by the chatter of machine guns: German fighter-bombers were strafing the long columns of refugees.

I leapt from my car and dived into the ditch. The time I spent in that uncomfortable position seemed endless, though the attack could only have lasted a minute or two. I emerged to find the road a scene of indescribable confusion: dead, wounded, overturned carts, scattered belongings, children sobbing, men and women in tears. It was my very first sight of the horrors of war. What made

14

it even more distressing was that all those involved were defenceless civilians — the soldiers were several kilometres away by this time. This frightful spectacle confirmed all that I had ever been told about war, and I drove on with a bitter taste in my mouth.

The road ahead was clearer — travelling by car I had overtaken the bulk of the refugees — so I got to Paris that evening. I found the 'city of light' shrouded in darkness, but some friends in the French capital quickly found me a room at a small hotel in Saint-Germain-des-Prés.

It was hard to believe, when I awoke the next morning, that I had come so close to death less than twenty-four hours earlier. Life went gaily on all around me. Carefree Parisians, young and old, were enjoying their morning coffee and croissants on the terrace of the Café Flore.

Anxious to rid my mind of the horrors I had seen, I spent two days seeking oblivion in cafés and nightclubs where hard liquor flowed like water and the girls were easy. It was a vain hope: harsh reality continually gained the upper hand.

15

The news from the north was very bleak. In Belgium King Leopold had surrendered unconditionally. The Yser line, scene of so many feats of arms during the First World War, was undefended. The remnants of the British Expeditionary Force had fallen back on Dunkirk. Fighting with their backs to the sea and exposed to incessant attacks from the air, they embarked for England in the motley assortment of ships and small craft that had been assembled on the other side of the Channel.

The most preposterous rumours were circulating in Paris, where a craze had developed for hunting spies alleged to have landed by parachute. That was how, while sharing a table at the Brasserie Lipp with a Flemish acquaintance from Antwerp and chatting with him in his native tongue, I came to be hauled off for interrogation and a rigorous identity check. The real enemy agents and fifth-columnists must have laughed their heads off at this mania for spy-hunting, because it was the Parisians themselves who had spread such rumours and sown the seeds of panic. Not a single enemy aircraft had overflown the city.

Feeling that I ought to make myself useful in some way, I went to the Dutch embassy to offer my services. There I was greeted by a bunch of army officers who seemed more interested in accumulating bottles of Scotch whisky than in helping a poor young devil who was eager to serve his country.

I left the embassy in a profoundly hurt and disillusioned frame of mind. Then came a surprise: an officer caught me up at the gate. His muddy tunic was adorned with a captain's three pips, his unshaven face gaunt with fatigue. 'I'm just leaving for England,' he told me. 'Sorry I can't take you along, but our car is overloaded as it is.' If I genuinely wanted to fight on like him and his companions, he said, I should make my way to Nantes or Bordeaux and try to get to England from there.

The French government quit Paris and moved to Bordeaux. The Germans were now at the gates of the capital, and there was nothing more I could do there. I still had a good stock of petrol, but I managed to supplement it with the help of friends, one of whom owned a garage in the suburb of Juvisy.

And so, as May, 1940, drew to a close, I decided to drive south to Marseilles and take refuge with the Reynauds, the family friends whom I had first encountered in Switzerland as a boy of five.

The trip from Paris to Marseilles went without a hitch. I parked my car in a side street running off the Boulevard Chave, rang the bell, and was welcomed with open arms. 'Kinou', the Reynauds' daughter, was only fourteen at the time. It never crossed my mind that one day, a uniformed survivor of the vicissitudes of war, I would ask her to marry me.

2

Provence: June, 1940 – January, 1941

I COULDN'T believe my eyes and ears. With the exception of a handful of realists, the French were living in a state of total apathy and unconcern. It was almost as if the war had left them untouched, or as if the débâcle had traumatized them to such an extent that their reactions were dulled.

German troops paraded down the Champs-Élysées. Paul Reynaud, the French premier, lost the support of the Bordeaux cabinet and the elderly Marshal Pétain proclaimed himself head of state with unlimited powers.

Winston Churchill, accompanied by the leaders of the Labour and Liberal parties and the three chiefs of staff, had arranged to meet Reynaud in Brittany on 16 June, 1940, to discuss the terms of an Anglo-French Union. The introductory paragraph of the draft proclamation was eloquent of the firm resolve of those who flatly refused to lie down under the German jackboot:

At this most fateful moment in the history of the modern world the Governments of the United Kingdom and the French Republic make this declaration of indissoluble union and unyielding resolution in their common defence of justice and freedom against subjection to a system which reduces mankind to a life of robots and slaves.

The Anglo-French meeting never took place: when Paul Reynaud submitted this proposal to his cabinet he was forced to resign. France's craven capitulation, which left the United Kingdom to carry the torch of freedom alone, sowed the seeds of the profound suspicion with which the British, Dutch, Norwegians and Poles, not to mention President Roosevelt, were to regard everything French in the years to come. Even General de Gaulle became an indirect victim of their mistrust.

'England, like Carthage, will be destroyed.' By rekindling ancient antagonisms dating from the time of Joan of Arc, German propaganda had done its work well. Insidiously, it boosted the reputation of Pétain, whom many French people still revered for his exploits at Verdun during the First World War.

It was announced on the radio that the Marshal had requested an armistice and conferred with Hitler at Montoire. France was cut in two. The Germans occupied the coastal regions from the English Channel to the Bay of Biscay and all French territory north of the Loire and west of the Swiss frontier, leaving their Italian allies to strut around on the shores of the Mediterranean.

A puppet government was set up at Vichy under the premiership of Pierre Laval, a man in the pay of Germany. Those who sought to fight on from the French possessions overseas or in metropolitan France itself were condemned to death *in absentia*.

This spirit of defeatism was not shared by the friends with whom I had taken refuge, and we had listened with great emotion to General de Gaulle's broadcast from London on 18 June. His steadfast attitude reinforced my own determination to join the forces that were carrying on the struggle.

The Dutch consul in Marseilles was loyal to our Queen, who had now formed a government-in-exile in London, and it was he who first introduced me to the Resistance.

Only Jean, my future father-in-law, suspected that I had embarked on this course. I got in touch with some people who were actively opposing measures taken by the Vichy police. One of them was a Belgian who administered the assets of Jewish refugees abroad. Although I was rather wary of the man, because he consorted with 'suspect' elements at Vichy including Otto Abetz, the German Ambassador, I played along with him and set up an escape route for Jews fleeing from the occupied territories.

One of the Belgian's contacts was Baron de Malval, a former Belgian Ambassador to London who had returned to France prior to May, 1940, and was living at the Villa Isabelle near Cannes.

There I met Commandant Paul Paillole, who was also planning to get to London, and it was through him that I made the acquaintance of Captains Marcel Chevance and Henri Frenay, both of whom were later to distinguish themselves in the Resistance. As a front for his clandestine activities, Chevance had set up a removals business near the Porte d'Aix in Marseilles.

The Plage des Catalans, a Marseilles beach, was an ideal spot for relaxation. I often visited it with Kinou and made a number of friends there. Most of the young men of my age who disported themselves on the beach were ex-members of the armed forces. Whether officially demobilized or not, they had refrained from returning to their homes in the occupied zone so as to avoid being drafted into the STO (Compulsory Labour Service).

The Plage des Catalans was where I recruited my first *résistants* and formed an embryonic network whose members included Paul Eckmann and Régine, a local 'madame'. No one was supposed to know about our clandestine activities.

In the bay was a large breakwater constructed of boulders, and it was there, having swum the two hundred metres that separated it from the shore, that we met to exchange information of all kinds and assess its relative importance. Our gleanings were then conveyed to London via Marcel Chevance and his channel of communication, a ship's officer who regularly plied between Marseilles and Casablanca.

It soon became apparent to me that our efforts were amateurish in the extreme. Secrecy was unknown and our members boasted openly of their exploits. The Vichy police were quickly alerted, no doubt, as were the Gestapo agents who abounded in Marseilles.

Paul Eckmann was arrested and detained at Fort Saint-Nicolas. Inspector Peretti, a well-disposed policeman who was present at Paul's preliminary interrogation, released him before the Gestapo intervened or any great harm could be done. Regretfully quitting his attic studio in the Vieux Port, Paul exchanged it for a temporary bolt-hole I found him in Régine's rue Estelle brothel.

Madame Régine was a loyal *résistante* with a weakness for the English. Ninochka, one of her girls, hid Paul in her room between 'tricks'. She was a delightful young Pole who had freely chosen the world's oldest profession as a means of saving up enough money to emigrate to Canada, the land of her dreams.

Not long afterwards, Paul decided to return to Roubaix, his family home near the Belgian frontier, and we suspended our activities on Inspector Peretti's advice.

★ ★ ★

It was now time to step up my own preparations for departure. The first essential was to obtain an exit visa from the authorities at Vichy. I knew that Allied nationals were interned in Spain if caught escaping, and rumours of the notorious detention camp at Miranda had already filtered across the Pyrenees. Miranda was where Gestapo agents selected those detainees who were to be brought back and incarcerated in German jails.

I still had my trusty Chevrolet, complete

with Pennsylvania licence plates, and a re-entry permit for the United States. This proved a considerable asset during my journey across Spain, because the United States had not yet entered the war. Myles Standish, the US vice-consul in Marseilles, was a great help to me. He and his boss, the American Ambassador at Vichy, were still *personae gratae* with the authorities there, and it was through them that I obtained my exit visa.

There remained the problem of how to get through Spain. I had vainly examined every other way of reaching Gibraltar or Lisbon. Several of us had even considered buying a yacht berthed in the Vieux Port. However, we should have had to pass through Spanish territorial waters on our way to Gibraltar, so this quixotic plan was abandoned.

A Barcelona family, the de Gallarts, had taken refuge with my sister in Austria during the Spanish Civil War, so they owed our family a favour. They repaid it in full when I contacted them. Rubio de Gallart was related to the Conde de Mayalde, Madrid's security chief. Thanks to his good offices, I finally obtained a

Spanish transit visa.

Meanwhile I was leading a normal life except when engaging in clandestine activities, but those occupied little of my time. Kinou, who considered me far too idle, regularly scolded me for not taking up arms against the enemy.

The Reynaud family had lent their weekend cottage in the hills above Aix-en-Provence to some Dutch friends whose seaside home at Èze had been requisitioned by the Italians. We used to hoist the Dutch and French flags when visiting them on Sundays. Concealed beneath some logs in a disused well near by was a cache of arms for the Resistance, carefully wrapped and greased.

Much of the locally grown food was shipped off to Germany, so the black market had made its appearance. A small cottage just above the Reynauds' served as a clandestine abattoir where calves, cows and other livestock were converted into joints of meat under cover of darkness. (even now, when gardening beside the party wall between the two properties, I occasionally unearth some of the bones that were buried there.)

At this stage the atmosphere in the South of France was still relatively calm and carefree, with few signs of the tribulations that lay ahead. The word from Brussels, which I received via my old nurse in Switzerland, was that my parents were as well and happy as could be expected under present circumstances. This was reassuring news. Less reassuring was the fact that the Vichy police were stepping up their activities.

It was time for me to leave.

3

Journey into the Unknown

THE documents I needed were slow to materialize. The exit visa I had obtained with such difficulty from Vichy would soon expire. Not only had I booked a passage to New York on a neutral ship — the *Siboney* of the Companhia Nacional de Navegação — due to leave Lisbon shortly but, more importantly, the Vichy police were already on our tails on account of the embryonic Resistance operations with which we were involved. Being now in a hurry to get away, I again enlisted the help of Myles Standish, the US vice-consul at the Château Pastré.

In return for a promise to destroy the document once it had got me through Spain, I was furnished with a typed declaration to the effect that the US authorities had granted me my 'first papers', and that I was technically an

American citizen. This, together with the fact that I was the owner-driver of a car registered in the United States, proved to be a great asset.

Although I had been unable to obtain a French *permis de circuler*, or driver's permit for the Chevvy, I still had enough petrol in reserve to get me from the Spanish frontier to Barcelona. The solution I devised was to load the car and trailer on to an old charcoal-burning lorry and transport them to the frontier.

My Spanish transit visa finally came through on 27 January, 1941. I hurried to the consulate to pick it up, and early the next morning, with all the neighbours looking on, the car and trailer were duly loaded. The lorry, which had not been requisitioned precisely because of its advanced age and decrepit condition, 'coughed' ominously. Its days were so evidently numbered that my worst fears soon came true: it conked out in the middle of Saint-Martin-de-Crau, less than 50 kilometres from Marseilles, and refused point-blank to start again.

Wind and rain combined to send my

morale, already low, plunging to rock-bottom. Faced with yet another dilemma, I decided that the only solution was to unload. I had enough petrol to get me across the frontier. Only time would tell what happened after that.

Anticipating such problems at Marseilles, I had fabricated a pink card that closely resembled a *permis de circuler*. Now was the time to use my forgery, so I affixed it to the windscreen. Although it looked convincing at a distance, I had to avoid a police check at all costs.

I abandoned the lorry in a ditch and set off again, this time at the wheel of my beloved Chevvy. The icy mistral was blowing harder than ever, and I passed one check-point without incident. Reluctant to venture out of their sentry-box because of the foul weather, the gendarmes merely waved me on. The sight of my 'permit' and an American car must have convinced them that I was a diplomat.

It had been dark for several hours when I finally reached Le Perthus. My battery had given up the ghost en route, and it was only by spending much time and even more money that I managed to acquire a replacement from a small garage in Perpignan. The border was closed for the night by the time I got there, so I took a room above a bistro called 'Chez Vidal'.

I was now confronted by a major problem: my French exit visa was valid only until midnight. How would I fare in the morning? I found that out at dawn the next day when I presented myself at the frontier post. The verdict was predictable: 'Your visa has expired. You'll have to apply to Vichy for an extension.'

The inspector, who was sent for, eyed me suspiciously and asked a number of questions. I told him the story of the lorry and explained that circumstances had compelled me to abandon it and drive on without a permit in the hope of reaching the frontier before the fateful hour when my visa ran out.

I sensed that I was in some danger, because it was probable that police headquarters had some inkling of my clandestine activities, so I produced the declaration given me by the American consulate. I was thereupon allowed to leave the post but told to remain at Le Perthus until my visa had been renewed. This, the inspector told me, would take some time. In the interim I must surrender my car keys. I had been condemned to immobility.

In the bistro that night I gathered from my slender knowledge of Catalan that I was in a smugglers' haunt — one that operated under the noses, and with the knowledge, of the local police and customs officers. I got into conversation with Vidal, the *patron*, and spun him enough of a yarn to convince him that I was a nephew of President Roosevelt's. Feeling that a person with such grand connections might be of future benefit to his clandestine business dealings, Vidal disclosed that there was a Gestapo officer at Le Perthus charged with supervising the activities of the French police.

To reinforce his idea of my own importance, I showed him the most recent telegram I had received at Marseilles from the Spanish security chief in Madrid. He advised me not to linger at Le Perthus, and my last hundred dollars clinched his decision to assist me.

It was freezing hard and snowing by this time, so Vidal advised me to ask the French frontier police to house my car and the trailer laden with my baggage in a nearby barn belonging to none other than Vidal himself. I would remain at Le Perthus for a few days only, just long enough to put the gendarmes off their guard. Meanwhile, I had to report to them twice a day.

Five days passed in this way. I was growing impatient, because the *Siboney*, on which I had booked a passage to New York, was scheduled to leave Lisbon on 7 February, only five days hence. What was more, bad news might arrive from Vichy.

Vidal's barn-cum-garage was situated less than a hundred metres from the frontier, which was sealed off at night with a length of chain. Double doors at the rear of the barn provided an exit for the agricultural machinery housed inside. That afternoon one of Vidal's friends hot-wired my car so that I could start it up without a key.

The entire village was asleep when two

shadowy figures emerged from the bistro at three the next morning. Vidal opened the rear doors, shifted the agricultural machinery, and I was free to leave.

Revving hard, I took off fast and covered the hundred metres to the frontier without lights. A jolt, and the chain snapped. I roared past the frontier post while the sentry was drinking coffee laced with rum provided by a smuggler friend of Vidal's, his customary bribe for turning a blind eye.

The Spanish frontier post came into view around a bend in the road. I would have to bluff my way through. The frontier guards spoke Catalan. I told them in Spanish to rouse their officer from his bed at once. It was essential to settle matters before the French cut up rough and demanded my return. If the Gestapo officer at Le Perthus got wind of the affair, it would be even worse for me.

Although I was kept under guard with a rifle levelled at my chest, I already felt safer. The officer, a tubby little man still struggling to buckle his belt, appeared at last. Bleary-eyed and thoroughly ill-tempered, unwashed and smelling of rancid olive oil, he was an officer nonetheless. The usual litany: '*Papeles? De dónde viene? Adónde va? Por qué razón?*'

Then the problem of my passport: '*Holandés?*' All Dutch nationals in Spain were subject to internment, I was told. So much for Spanish 'neutrality'!

Attack being the best method of defence, I harangued the man in Spanish: 'You see these papers from the consulate? I'm technically an American national. Here's my Spanish transit visa — it's perfectly valid. I'm a personal friend of the Conde de Mayalde and the Marqués de Camarasa, military governor of the province of San Sebastián. What do you think they'll say if they hear that some incompetent pipsqueak of a Guardia Civil has sent me back to France?'

That threw the officer, who now looked uneasy. Only someone with connections would have dared to address him in such a manner. Having examined my visa, more carefully this time, he agreed that it was valid, but only for the frontier post at Irún and the road to San Sebastián, and pointed out that he had not been forewarned of my arrival. I explained that I had chosen the shortest route because my French exit visa was about to expire.

In the end I was told to drive the car and trailer to the barracks in the next village, where the officer himself was stationed, and remain there until he obtained authorization from Madrid.

My reference to the Conde and the Marqués had impressed him, however. When a French delegation turned up to retrieve me on the grounds that I had crossed the frontier illegally and damaged government property in the process, he sent them packing. I was now under Spanish protection, he declared, and if they wanted to see me again they would have to submit a formal request for extradition to the authorities in Madrid.

I was permitted to telephone my friends in Barcelona, who did their best to put a squib under the Ministry of the Interior. The wheels of Spanish officialdom, too, turned very slowly, so the five ensuing days were spent in a state of suspended animation. Meantime, I and José, the plump little officer, became the best of friends.

It was late one cold, snowy afternoon when José sent me on my way with a cordial '*Hasta la vista*'. I knew, alas, that the *Siboney* had long since left Lisbon and was already ploughing her way across the North Atlantic.

I headed for my destination along winding Spanish roads. My friends lived in Horta, a southern suburb of Barcelona. A resplendent moon was shining by the time I sighted 'Las Euras', their big white villa among the hills, and it was almost ten o'clock when I drove through the majestic gateway and up the tree-lined drive. I rang the bell. A butler answered the door, but before he could announce me Señora de Gallart welcomed me with open arms.

Forgetting what late hours the Spaniards keep, I apologized profusely for my belated arrival, only to have my hostess tell me, 'Go and freshen up, then join us in the *salón*. We dine at eleven.'

I dispelled my weariness by wallowing in a good, hot bath, then snatched a moment to admire the view from my balcony. Below me, against a background of moon-gilded sea, Barcelona stretched away into the distance like a dark robe sprinkled with thousands of tiny sequins. To one accustomed to the French blackout it seemed a doubly glorious sight and I could have feasted my eyes on it for ever.

My visa specified Valencia de Alcántara as my point of egress from Spain. Señor de Gallart advised me to take the southern road to Zaragoza, this being further from the frontier zone and the Guardia Civil patrols that kept it under surveillance. He also had some new car keys cut and undertook to provide me with enough petrol to get me to Lisbon. Resisting the temptation to stay on for a few days, as I was warmly invited to do, I set off again the next day.

It was almost dark by the time I crossed the Ebro bridge at Zaragoza, so I decided to spend the night there. I parked my car and trailer in the square outside police headquarters, having first obtained permission to do so from the policeman on duty, who assured me that he would keep an eye on them.

The hotel porter called me at dawn and made me some coffee, which I drank in the kitchen before going off to collect my car. To my alarm I found that the trailer's tarpaulin cover had been disturbed: my cans of petrol were gone, presumably stolen by someone who had seen me topping up my tank the previous night. The police disclaimed all knowledge of the theft, naturally, so I was compelled to regard it as a form of toll fee. This necessitated a complete change of plan. I was now perilously short of money, having spent my hundred-dollar nest-egg on getting out of Le Perthus, so I decided to head for Madrid and seek help there from the parents of a friend of mine, Pablo Wirth-Lenaerts.

I drove to the Spanish capital by way of Guadalajara, the scene of fierce fighting during the Spanish Civil War. Pablo was away from home, as I already knew, but his parents insisted on putting me up for the night and fixed me an appointment with the Conde de Mayalde, who had gone to such lengths to get me my visa. They also gave me enough Spanish money to get me to Lisbon.

A tall, imposing man, Mayalde was a true hidalgo who might have stepped out of the pages of Cervantes. An aristocrat to his fingertips and somewhat haughty in the manner of a Spanish grandee, he bore the impress of his country's great past. He knew my sister and her Austrian husband and was very concerned about what had happened to them. Although he and his family supported General Franco, they had little time for the Germans. He also had little respect for the French and distrusted the British, though my dealings with him were facilitated by his almost perfect command of English, which he spoke with an exquisite Oxford accent.

It was raining hard when I left Madrid, so I saw little of the Spanish countryside as I drove via Talavera de la Reina, Plasencia and Cáceres to Valencia de Alcántara. A frontier town, Valencia was thick with check-points, and Pablo's father had advised me to avoid them by taking a minor road that led straight to the frontier. This road, which ran through undulating fields, proved to be an unsurfaced farm track, and the persistent rain had made it very slippery.

In my eagerness to get across the frontier by nightfall, I speeded up. Before long I was confronted by an unexpected bend, a steep slope, and, at its foot, a small bridge spanning a ditch. Propelled by the weight of its trailer, the Chevvy skidded off the road when I braked. My only recourse was to accelerate and hope to clear the ditch. I succeeded, though the car turned a complete somersault before coming to rest.

The trailer, which had snapped its coupling, remained on the other side of the ditch. I myself had escaped with a few bruises and a bloody nose. I got out and took stock of the situation. Miraculously, the engine and wheels were still functional — not even the steering had suffered from the impact, and the windows and windscreen were intact. A peasant who had witnessed the incident in the distance came hurrying to the scene with his ox. The ox proved invaluable. Harnessed to the front bumper, it managed to haul the car back on to the road.

The trailer, however, was a write-off. I transferred as many of my belongings as possible to the already overloaded Chevvy and made the delighted peasant a gift of the trailer and its remaining contents. He bade me a cordial '*Adiós*' and shook my hand warmly. This gesture surprised me, because it seemed a little at odds with his otherwise dour demeanour.

It wasn't until I had crossed the Portuguese frontier and checked into a small hotel at Marvão that the reason for his cordiality dawned on me. I discovered when I came to wash my hands that my gold ring with inset diamond, a gift from my mother, had vanished. Counting the petrol stolen by the police at Zaragoza, this was the second fee I'd paid the Spaniards for the privilege of traversing their country.

The news next morning was far from promising. Fate seemed to be against me because the main road to Lisbon was closed: the bridges over the Tagus had been carried away by floods. I would be obliged to travel via Évora and take a ferry across to Lisbon.

It was late afternoon when I reached Évora, a prosperous little town, so I decided to spend the night there. The hotel was a two-storeyed building with a large central courtyard and rooms running off the open gallery that enclosed it. The receptionist announced that the only room available was 'the best' and assured me that an English queen — presumably Queen Victoria — had slept there. My quarters turned out to be a vast chamber with a big four-poster and velvet drapes. Weary but feeling good, now that no more policemen or frontier guards would haunt my dreams, I retired to bed immediately after dinner.

The storm continued to rage outside, buffeting the shutters like repeated blows from a clenched fist. The electricity supply failed, so a maid brought me an oil lamp and a candle. I snuggled down under the bedclothes, which were surmounted by a thick eiderdown, and went to sleep.

Soon afterwards I was jolted awake by a terrible crash. I groped for the matches, lit the oil lamp, and was confronted by an alarming sight. Toppled by the wind, an entire chimney had fallen through the ceiling and landed on the floor beside me. In view of the debris that littered the canopy of the four-poster and the bed itself, I blessed the thickness of the eiderdown.

After spending the rest of the night in an armchair in the hotel lounge, I learned that Portugal had been devastated by a hurricane. The greatest natural disaster in living memory, it had left a trail of death and destruction in its wake.

I reached the Tagus by a roundabout route and managed to board the only ferry still operating, all the others having been sunk or driven ashore by the storm. Lisbon was only just across the water, but I had to leave the Chevvy behind because I didn't have enough cash for a car fare.

Armed with a single suitcase, I checked into a modest Lisbon hotel and then betook myself to the Dutch embassy where I inquired how best to get to England or Gibraltar. Although the response was negative, I did extract enough escudos from the embassy's emergency fund to cover the cost of two telegrams to the United States.

They both bore fruit the very next day. A Boston friend, Bob Harkness, wired me enough money to live on in Lisbon until I could obtain a berth aboard a ship bound for the States. More surprisingly, the hotel porter called to say that a liveried chauffeur was waiting to collect me and my baggage. When I asked for my bill, he told me that it had just been paid.

Any remaining doubts I had were dispelled by the sight of the discreet logo adorning the limousine outside. It belonged to the New York-based Shell Union Corporation, of which my brother's father-in-law was president, and the telegram announcing my arrival in Lisbon had evidently spurred him into action.

The chauffeur dropped me at the Hotel Palácio in Estoril, where a room had been booked for me. This luxurious establishment was well beyond my means, and I wondered how I would ever pay the bill. The chauffeur, who spoke English, told me that his boss, the oil company's local director, would meet me in the bar that evening.

I had a decent suit in my solitary suitcase, so I bathed and changed before keeping this appointment. My benefactor turned out to be a plump little Portuguese

46

named da Costa. Although Senhor da Costa lacked the majestic bearing of the Conde de Mayalde, his social status was apparent from the restrained cut of his well-tailored suit. He also spoke excellent English and French, which helped to break the ice. 'Don't worry,' he told me, promptly divining my thoughts, 'I've received instructions about you.' Having heard my story, he asked for the keys to my car and promised to send someone to collect it.

A peculiar atmosphere reigned at the Palácio, which would have made a perfect location for a James Bond film. The clientèle, an international bunch, seemed to spend much of the time spying on each other. Although I was one of the youngest residents, I fitted in with ease and made some enjoyable excursions to neighbouring places of interest such as Belém, Sintra and the Bôca do Inferno.

I was often visited by my new-found friend and benefactor, who introduced me to his circle of acquaintances. It was his habit at night to go to the casino, which was situated opposite the hotel, and play a few hands of bridge. On one occasion he invited me to accompany him. I accepted with pleasure, quite ignorant of how much a point he and his friends played for.

There were four tables in use that night. It was eleven by the casino clock when the session began and five in the morning when it ended. Although I was an inexperienced player and changed partners three times, I never lost a hand. It would have been bad form to bow out — winners don't do that in polite society — so I cleared enough in that one night to cover all my living expenses and pay for my own and my car's passage to the States. What was more, I landed in New York with just over five hundred dollars in my wallet.

I have never again ventured into a casino without knowing how high the stakes are. To this day I don't know if it was Senhor da Costa's graceful way of assisting a young man without making him feel indebted. Latins can be very subtle when points of honour are involved!

The *Serpa Pinto*, an old liner owned by the Companhia Colonial de Navegação, carried some three hundred passengers in normal times. On this occasion two sections of the hold had been converted into dormitories, and eleven hundred crowded aboard. It was only nine months since I had heard Jewish refugees at Antwerp complain about sleeping four to a two-berth cabin. If they had been prepared to accept less comfortable quarters, many more of them might have escaped death at the hands of the Nazis.

The weather was now set fair and our route took us via the Azores. Protected by the flag of Portugal, a neutral country, the *Serpa Pinto* steamed across the Atlantic with all her lights blazing. As an ex-employee of the Holland America Line, I enjoyed certain privileges. The captain granted me access to the poop deck and boat deck, so the voyage was a treat from my point of view. By day I basked in the sun; at night, wrapped in a blanket, I slept on deck, far from the fug and stench of the makeshift dormitory where I had spent my first night aboard.

Nine days went by, and then, in the first light of dawn, we passed Nantucket lighthouse. Before long other familiar features came into view: the skyscrapers of Manhattan, the Statue of Liberty, the Hudson River, the wharfs of Hoboken.

Old Europe and its warlike clamour seemed a million miles away, but I couldn't help thinking of the friends I'd left behind, some of whom were in constant peril of their lives.

4

The Star-Spangled Banner and the Maple Leaf

IT took some time to complete the customs formalities and get my car unloaded. I had been unable to notify my date of arrival in advance, so no one was expecting me, but I knew my way around. I climbed into the overloaded Chevvy and headed for Manhattan along the Pulasky Skyway. En route I caught a distant glimpse of the burned-out hulk of the *Normandie*, to my mind the handsomest of all the great transatlantic liners.

I checked into the New Weston, a hotel well known to me because I had stayed there many times, on the last occasion prior to my departure for Europe in August, 1939. The head porter, who recognized me at once, was a Belgian whose parents still lived in Ostend. Understandably worried about them,

51

he joined me in the lounge when he came off duty and insisted on hearing a detailed account of conditions in occupied territory. I was agreeably surprised by the flowers and magnum of champagne that appeared in my room the next day, with the compliments of the management. It was a good omen and a pleasant introduction to the three months I spent in the United States.

My brother's father- and mother-in-law were a wonderful, warm-hearted couple. They promptly invited me to stay at their Long Island home, which became my base for visits to other friends in New England and Philadelphia.

I was disappointed by the general level of ignorance and unconcern prevailing in the United States. Having lived there for several years, I had felt confident that I understood the Americans. Now that I had acquired personal or vicarious experience of the war in Europe and the atrocities being perpetrated there, however, I was baffled by their complete detachment from and lack of interest in what was happening on the other side of the Atlantic. Although many of them were separated from their European roots by less than a generation, they buried their heads in the sand and blinded themselves to the truth. Who knows how many thousands of lives might have been saved had they entered the war sooner? As it was, the indecision and isolationism rife among their leading politicians — President Roosevelt excepted — were a positive incitement to the Japanese to go to war.

One of my old acquaintances, who taught at Princeton University, asked me to give a talk on the problems confronting patriots in occupied Europe and the abuses committed there by the invaders. My remarks were very coldly received, and I was not surprised when American newspapers questioned the truth of my statements. (I was belatedly vindicated in 1947, when one of the students present at my lecture got in touch with me. Having witnessed the horrors of the concentration camps at first hand while serving in the US Army, he felt ashamed that he had booed me, like many of his fellow students, as I left the lecture hall. Far better late than never, his admission consoled me at a time when I was still feeling thoroughly depressed.)

* * *

I eventually discovered that a unit of the Netherlands armed forces was being formed in Canada. It seemed obvious that my best way of fulfilling the task I had set myself — to get to England to assist in liberating my country — would be to join this unit as a volunteer. I applied to the consulate-general in New York and received my marching orders in mid-June: they instructed me to present myself at Stratford, Ontario, on 2 July.

I was about to attain my preliminary goal, which was to put on uniform and prepare to make an active contribution to the fight against Nazism. The Dutch national motto, *Je maintiendrai* (I shall uphold), steeled me for the road that lay ahead, which I guessed would be long and fraught with danger. My decision to follow that road had really been taken outside Noyon, when the Germans machine-gunned those defenceless refugees.

★ ★ ★

My new abode, Lagan Barracks, was a disused textile factory on the outskirts of Stratford. Its façade was now adorned with the words 'Princess Juliana Barracks'. Dutch volunteers eager to serve their country under the banner of the House of Orange had flocked there from many parts of the world including Asia, South Africa, Brazil, Curaçao and Surinam. One had even escaped from Holland by sea and joined the unit by way of Finland and Sweden. Most of our instructors were members of the Netherlands police who had fled to England before the capitulation.

Some eighty of us joined up on 2 July. Our first task was to sew the unit's insignia on our battledress sleeves. We were also issued with a maple leaf badge, the symbol of the country in which we had enlisted. Never having had to do military service, because I was foreign-born and had lived abroad all my life, I was not unnaturally assigned the lowly rank of private.

The first few days were taken up

55

with vaccinations, foot drill and learning how to handle our rifles, which were antiquated Lee-Enfields. We were also divided up into groups and encouraged to get to know our officers, who were reservists and had, like the rest of us, converged on Stratford from all over the world.

The pace of training gradually accelerated as time went by. Being unused to so much physical exertion, we ended the day exhausted, flat out on our beds and more than ready for a well-deserved night's rest — not that we always got one. Many were the times when, having just gone to sleep, we were routed out of bed and sent off on a night exercise.

The equipment made available to us by the Canadian Army was pitiable: rifles dating from the First World War, an equally ancient machine gun, and mortars that proved more dangerous to us than to any potential foe. Fortunately our military attaché in the United States managed to provide us with a few less obsolete weapons. Being a good shot, I inherited a fine new rifle with a telescopic sight, though I had to share it with my comrades during target practice.

The weeks passed quickly and we were allowed plenty of time off. We took full advantage of it, the one condition being that we caused no trouble in the town and turned out punctually on parade. This we sometimes failed to do, because many of us found ourselves girl-friends in the neighbourhood. We were highly sought-after in Stratford because we tended to have more money than the local boys, who regarded us as toy soldiers and were resentful of our amatory successes.

The inevitable happened one night when we were bold enough to invade a bar frequented by Canadian soldiers. They accused us of being 'overpaid, oversexed and over here', with the result that battle was joined in the forecourt of the establishment. By the time the MPs arrived we had won by force of numbers and disappeared into the darkness.

Illicit nocturnal forays were relatively easy to arrange with the help of room-mates who covered for us and ensured that our beds looked occupied. Our own spells of guard duty had taught us how to sneak in and out of barracks unobserved. All that could floor us was an unexpected muster parade. The worst thing was having to mount guard after one of these boozy escapades. Staying awake was a major problem, and I often pricked the underside of my chin when propping it on the tip of my bayonet to stop myself falling asleep.

International rivalry sometimes reared its head. The Canadian soldiers, who were in better training, challenged us to climb the water-tower near our barracks and plant a flag on top. The honour of the unit was at stake, so we quietly scaled the steel and concrete structure under cover of darkness. The inhabitants of Stratford were surprised the next morning to see an orange flag fluttering from the summit of the water-tower, together with a banner bearing the inscription 'WE'RE NO SISSIES!' I had planted the flag while some fellow recruits affixed the banner.

This exploit caused a sensation. Although extremely annoyed at first, our Commanding Officer took a lenient view of the affair when we explained about the challenge. We got off with a reprimand and an extra spell of guard duty. The local newspaper applauded our daring and the Canadians never threw down the gauntlet again.

Being the sole possessor of a car, I was much in demand with my comrades. Often dangerously overloaded, the Chevvy took us on numerous excursions to Toronto, Hamilton and Windsor, whence the skyscrapers of Detroit could be seen looming up beyond the waterway that links Lakes Erie and Huron.

My most enjoyable memory is of a few days' leave spent among the Muskoka Lakes, north of Toronto. Autumn comes quite early in that region, which extends all the way into the Far North, and the birch and larch forests were a sea of red and gold. The landscape was just as it must have appeared to the first trappers who set eyes on it, the only signs of civilization being the roads, few of which were asphalted, and an occasional log cabin. The sun was still hot enough for us to enjoy swimming in the sapphire waters of the district's many small lakes.

Another pleasant memory is of Princess Juliana of the Netherlands and her children, who had been sent to Canada to escape the London blitz. The Princess not only visited our barracks but was often entertained at their Toronto home by a Dutch family who were friends of my brother-in-law. On one occasion they invited me and a comrade of mine to have tea with her. Tea 'spilled over' into supper, and it was late when we finally took our leave. The Princess did not stand on ceremony. Chatting with complete informality, she asked me a number of very searching questions about my time in France, the Resistance activities I had already engaged in there, and my escape. She also laughed heartily at the story of my tribulations on the way to Lisbon. Much impressed by her knowledge of what was happening in poor, tormented Europe, I came away heartened by this chance encounter with our future queen.

The first snow had fallen by the time our date of departure drew near. Our Canadian hosts were busy preparing for the winter, we for our great adventure. We posed for group photographs and held a passing-out parade attended by the CO and sundry local dignitaries. At last, on 4 October, 1941, the train that was to transport us to the coast pulled into Stratford station.

It was snowing hard when we piled into the two carriages reserved for us, the remainder being occupied by some very boisterous Canadians. It was my job, as a member of No. 4 Platoon, to ensure that all our number were safely aboard and shut the doors. We hadn't been informed of our destination, but I guessed that it must be Halifax.

Slowly the train got under way and headed for Toronto. At Montreal we were allowed to stretch our legs and provided with mugs of hot tea by the military canteen installed on the platform. It was dark when we moved on, and we whiled away the time sleeping or playing cards. The train rattled through Quebec without stopping. By daybreak the character of the countryside had changed. We were in a broad, undulating plain dotted with little white farmhouses that glittered like jewels in the light of the rising sun. It was the Gaspé Peninsula, where we hitched on some additional carriages before heading south for Halifax.

The train finally slowed and came to a halt. Funnels, masts and cranes could be seen jutting above the roofs of the warehouses beside the track. We were scheduled to embark the next day. That meant spending another night aboard the train, but one of the warehouses had been converted into a canteen run by some pretty ATS girls, who cooked us a very welcome meal.

Our ship was the Capetown Castle, a Union Castle liner that had plied between Southampton and South Africa before the war. My father, who had made an extended cruise aboard her some ten years earlier, never dreamed that she would one day transport his younger son across the North Atlantic in time of war.

We embarked on 6 October, 1941. Peering out of the porthole of the cabin I shared with four others, No. 260 on C Deck, I saw two French liners berthed elsewhere in the harbour: the *De Grasse* and another ship whose familiar silhouette led me to identify her as the *Champollion*. When we cast off on Thursday morning, they followed us out of port flying the Croix de Lorraine — my first sight of the Free French colours so dear to my heart.

We began by hugging the coast. The convoy, some twenty vessels of all shapes and sizes, including freighters and tankers, gradually took up station as the day wore on and we headed out into deeper water. We also sighted a cruiser and nine vigilant destroyers. From time to time Catalina flying-boats of the Canadian Air Force circled in the sky above our heads.

With the cruiser in the lead and the destroyers on either flank, the ships maintained a distance of about a quarter of a mile. The convoy's speed was governed by its slowest member, but we noticed as the days went by that there were one or two persistent stragglers. We darkened ship completely at night and it was strictly forbidden to smoke on deck or carry a flashlight.

We followed a seemingly erratic route, often changing course for no apparent reason. One thing was certain: we were heading further north. Although this presented a danger of icebergs, we were given to understand that the risk was outweighed by other considerations. Not only were U-boats averse to operating in ice-infested waters, but air cover could be maintained for longer periods the nearer we got to Iceland. It was probable that some of the freighters in the convoy would peel off there and make for Murmansk.

Tension on board steadily mounted. Boat drills and compulsory physical training sessions did little to occupy the mind. Some of the men grew bored and curdled each other's blood telling scare stories. I, who loved the sea, steered clear of these prophets of doom.

On our fifth day out we heard the ships' sirens emit the series of short blasts that signalled an alert. We had to don our life-jackets and assemble in our cabins. Taking it in turns to look through the porthole, we saw the destroyers dashing to and fro like sheepdogs rounding up a flock. This, together with our ship's zigzag course, made it seem certain that some of Admiral Doenitz's dreaded U-boats were on the prowl.

Towards evening we heard, far astern of us, the characteristic thud of depth charges, followed by a violent explosion. It was caused by one of the stragglers, a freighter laden with ammunition. We all fell silent, thinking of the brave men who had just been swallowed up by the cold, grey Atlantic. No widows would ever mourn beside their watery grave.

The reappearance of air cover indicated that we must be nearing land and on 17 October we sailed into Liverpool. Our voyage was over. The vague feeling that we were impotent pawns of fate had left us at last.

5

The Princess Irene Brigade

NATIONAL units drawn from countries under German occupation were being formed and trained all over England. The Netherlands forces had set up their headquarters at Wrottesley Park, near Wolverhampton, and three coaches were waiting to take us there when we disembarked. Having loaded our kit into the trucks that brought up the rear, we 'embussed'. To most of our number the sight of a bomb-damaged city was a revelation. Liverpool and its neighbouring port, Birkenhead, were striking examples of the barbarism to which civilian populations had been subjected by the Germans.

The journey by road took only a few hours and it was early afternoon when we drove into camp. Loaded down with our belongings, we moved into the two wooden huts that were to serve as our temporary quarters. The cookhouse produced an ample evening meal and we followed it up with a good night's sleep.

Some welcome sunshine attended our first reveille in England. We were happy to have attained our first objective but had yet to get our bearings, so the morning parade was a chaotic affair. We spent the day waiting to have our particulars taken. Since this was done in alphabetical order, I was one of the last to be registered.

The next morning we were split up and assigned to existing units. Although I naturally had to turn out for drill and guard duty, I was fortunate enough to have been appointed honorary 'administrative head' of my section. This exempted me from fatigues such as potato-peeling and latrine-cleaning. I even had a cubicle of my own, like an NCO.

At this stage the 'brigade' had an effective strength of approximately eleven hundred men, over two hundred of whom were officers of various ranks. This glaring disproportion was attributable to the fact that more officers than other ranks had contrived to escape to England. Our equipment, which was modern, consisted of armoured cars, Bren-gun carriers, three-tonners, and all that was needed to equip an infantry unit. Training was far more rigorous than in Canada, but it helped to alleviate the monotony of life in camp as the year drew to a close and 1942 dawned.

Convinced that the liberation of Europe was a relatively distant prospect, we were delighted to hear that volunteers could apply to be sent to Burma for infiltration into the Dutch East Indies. That was how I came to learn Malay, the lingua franca of the area. I asked a friend in London to get me a Berlitz course on gramophone records, and a small party of us used to congregate in my room at night to improve our knowledge of the language, which was essential for acceptance. Sadly, this project had to be abandoned because the Japanese had already penetrated too far into Burma. We were all so deeply disappointed that the boredom of camp life weighed twice as heavily thereafter, though I myself was fortunate enough to have certain outside distractions.

Tettenhall was a small town some fifteen minutes' walk from our camp, and it was at the YMCA canteen there that I got to know several young WAAFs based at Bridgnorth, a neighbouring fighter station. One of them, Sibyl, happened to be the daughter of some people I knew in London. As a friend of Sibyl's and a foreigner who had escaped from Europe, I was adopted by the wing-commander in charge of the fighter station, who gave me special permission to patronize the pub midway between our camp and Bridgnorth, which was out of bounds to all but RAF personnel. This I did in a uniform acquired while on leave in London, a Savile Row confection tailored in the same barathea as an officer's service dress, so all I lacked were the pips and Sam Browne belt. I spent many enjoyable evenings in the company of Sibyl and her fighter pilot friends, whose squadron had distinguished itself during the Battle of Britain. All that remained after each such 'sortie' was to sneak back into camp behind the guardhouse and regain my hut unobserved. My previous experience at Stratford stood me in good stead and I was only caught on one occasion — an offence that earned me three days' confinement to barracks.

At the end of January I and a few others, including my friend John Steengracht van Mooyland, were summoned to the CO's office and informed that our academic qualifications fitted us for officer training at Camberley. John and I declined this offer. We hadn't come to England to swell the ranks of the two hundred Dutch officers waiting to parade through the streets of The Hague when our country was finally liberated. Even if it meant passing up a second-lieutenant's pip, we preferred a more active role.

This revolt against the established order had salutary consequences from our point of view. We were sent for by the Inspector-General of the Netherlands Armed Forces, General Noothoven van Goor, who lived in a large country house near the camp. A pleasant man of retirement age, he asked us some extremely pertinent questions and listened to our replies with close attention. He evidently sympathized with our desire to make ourselves useful in an operational role as soon as possible, because he assured us before we left that he would do his best to fulfil it.

6

Preparing for the Real Thing

IT was the experience gained by General Sir Dudley Clarke during the Boer War and in Palestine that prompted Winston Churchill, on becoming Prime Minster, to create certain units analogous to German storm troops. Initially designated Special Service Battalions, these independent units became No. 1 Commando. They had previously seen action in Norway under the command of Lord Lovat, who ran them like a private army divorced from War Office control.

The Household Division, London District and Eastern Command supplied the basic personnel of three other units that bore the name 'Commandos' and the total was increased to eleven when Scottish, Southern and Western Commands each supplied two more units.

No. 12 Commando, which was formed in August, 1941, consisted of men from Northern Ireland, but No. 10 Commando did not come into being until June, 1942. The number remained a mere cipher until then because Northern Command had failed to raise a sufficient number of volunteers. By the war's end there were some twenty commandos in existence.

For security reasons I was ordered when leaving Wrottesley Park to state that I had been posted to London, although my movement order was made out for Carlisle in the far north-west. My only luggage was a kitbag; the rest, I was assured, would follow on.

Met at Carlisle station by a sergeant in the Military Police, I found when I reached the camp that it was a military prison. I wondered aloud what I'd done to deserve such a fate, but to no avail; the sergeant left my questions unanswered.

I was tucked away in a guardroom and issued with a new uniform adorned with Pioneer Corps shoulder flashes. Having put this on, I was photographed and given a new paybook and identity disc. My name had been changed: I was now 'Guy Shreve' [sic].

At last an officer appeared. He told me that I had been assigned to 'special operations' and that, although he had no idea what this entailed, I was to hold myself in readiness to leave in an hour's time for Thurso in the north of Scotland. I was also sworn to absolute secrecy about my mission, whatever it might be.

The headquarters at Thurso consisted of a large house standing in its own grounds. There were no huts, all personnel being accommodated in the main building. After undergoing another thorough interrogation, I was informed that I now belonged to one of the Special Service Battalions commanded by Lord Lovat. Most of my fellow trainees I identified as Scottish by their broad accents, but there were also a few Norwegians and one French survivor of the Norwegian campaign.

Training, especially at night, was arduous in the extreme. I had my first introduction to amphibious landings in motor torpedo boats, which were commanded by Norwegians and a few British officers. The water was icy cold

74

in early March, but we had to wade through it regardless. One feature of these landing exercises was the hail of bullets that whistled over our heads as instructors fired their Bren guns in our direction, using live ammunition. We very soon learned how to hug the ground and take cover behind every little mound of stones. The instructors tried to halt our advance and the secret was to outflank their firing points and pelt them with thunderflashes. We ourselves were not entitled to use live ammunition, so I had no chance to demonstrate my prowess as a marksman. One of our advantages as attackers was that the tracer bullets betrayed their source and enabled us to locate 'enemy' positions. Absolute self-discipline was essential on such occasions and we acquired a mastery of movement and speed of reaction for which I was more than grateful in the future.

It was bliss, after these exercises, to climb into bed and snatch a few hours' sleep. Still exhausted, we had to turn out on parade next morning freshly shaved with our uniforms and equipment in spotless condition, grateful to the chill of the Scottish dawn for keeping us awake.

I had been assigned to 'HQ Group' in the capacity of interpreter and marksman, and was itching to see some action. Rumour had it that our unit was to be incorporated in the newly-formed commandos, but the days went by and nothing happened. Before we left, Lord Lovat wished us good luck and disclosed that the task for which we had been earmarked — a raid on the south coast of Norway coupled with a diversionary attack on one of the Frisian Islands — had definitely been cancelled. I myself would have taken part in the latter operation.

After seventeen strenuous days at Thurso I was posted to a training camp under construction at Achnacarry on the shores of Loch Lochy, south of Loch Ness. A Royal Engineers unit was already at work on it and we had to assist them in constructing huts and assault courses. It must have been considered a matter of great urgency because we even worked at night in the glare of arc lamps — a highly exceptional proceeding in a country where the blackout was normally universal. A week later I was sent south once more, catching a glimpse of Ben Nevis and stopping at Fort William en route.

No. 12 Commando had based itself at Dunoon on the Firth of Clyde, the epicentre of all these crack units. When I arrived there in March, 1942, the following units were already established in the area: No. 3 Commando at Largs, No. 2 Commando at Troon, and No. 9 Commando on the Island of Bute. There were various other formations at Rothesay, Ayr and Irvine. Some French marines had been assigned to the commando at Troon, and I was delighted to find, when I joined No. 12 Commando, that some other Dutchmen had been posted there. Among them was my friend John Steengracht, who had witnessed my departure from Tettenhall with envy. They all thought I was in London, so they were surprised to see me again. Remembering my debt to security, I merely told them that I had undergone some preliminary training at Achnacarry.

The commando consisted mainly of men from Northern Ireland. Noisy and bibulous, they had little love for the English, so foreigners like us were readily assimilated into their ranks. We were soon packed off to Achnacarry, my previous port of call, for two weeks' intensive training.

The tortuous, windswept road took us past the snow-capped summits of Ben Nevis and Craig Megaidh to Spean Bridge and the deep, dark waters of Loch Arkaig and Loch Lochy. The area wasn't new to me, of course, but nothing had prepared me for the rigours of the training we underwent there, nor for the transformation that had taken place since my last sight of Achnacarry Camp. A dozen Nissen huts and a large central building had sprouted from the mud in the intervening month.

Achnacarry was a merciless test of endurance designed to eliminate anyone physically or mentally below par. I heard from subsequent 'graduates' that changes had had to be introduced because of excessive wastage!

It was still dark on the morrow of

our arrival when we set off on our first forced march: twenty kilometres at the double in full equipment, and this was just a foretaste of the delights in store. The assault course that awaited us was diabolical. For four kilometres we scrambled up and down rocks, launched ourselves into space and landed on ankle-twisting turf, skinned our hands and knees while crawling along concrete pipes just wide enough to admit a man's body, waded through mountain torrents with or without hand-ropes, scaled log walls, and negotiated countless obstacles. In addition we were required to engage moving targets with our personal weapons at various points on the course. Our weapons, which became clogged with sandy soil if we failed to keep them above our heads, had to be cleaned with numb fingers, often in the dark. No easy matter, this lost us precious time and reduced the points we scored, which would determine whether we remained commandos or were sentenced to be RTUed (returned to unit).

Will-power and perseverance were all that could enable one to withstand the inhuman exertions demanded by this course of training and stick it out to the bitter end. The reason for its severity, I learned later, was that we were intended to become the instructors of those who formed the nucleus of all commando units, even including the US Rangers.

It was this inculcation of unquestioning obedience and steadfast resolve, respect for one's comrades and acceptance of danger, that produced the men who acquitted themselves so gallantly during the commando raids and other operations that helped to liberate our native lands.

From my own point of view the course was an ordeal by fire. In conjunction with what I was later taught at the schools run by SOE, it fitted me to carry out my subsequent mission in occupied territory and survive the Nazi concentration camps. That is why I still feel so grateful to the officers and NCOs whom I sometimes regarded, when I lay slumped on my bed in a state of utter exhaustion, as wanton torturers.

★ ★ ★

Clydebank, Glasgow's seaport, had suffered badly from the German bombing. All its inhabitants had been evacuated, leaving it a rubble-strewn ghost town. The shipyards that had once been its pride and joy were at a standstill and the long thoroughfares, flanked by gutted houses and factories, constituted a sombre image of the horrors of war. Out of bounds to civilians, this district had been taken over as a training area where commandos were initiated into the art of street-fighting. The existing devastation was such that the whole quarter had to be razed to the ground and rebuilt after the war, so any resulting damage was immaterial.

The essence of street-fighting technique was to advance in small teams or pairs, of which John Steengracht and I formed one. Sneaking like rats from house to house, room to room, cellar to cellar, we climbed ruined staircases, broke down doors, smashed windows and covered each other as we darted from one building to the next or gained access by way of backyards or roofs. We would often get from one house to another by blowing a hole in the party wall with explosives.

In the interests of realism, we had to dislodge 'enemy' forces made up of Home Guard units reinforced by instructors and commando marksmen. The object of such exercises was to clear every house or ruined building in the area. Although they were only war games, the setting in which they took place and the seriousness with which we played them approximated to reality. Umpires decreed which of us had been killed or wounded, and prisoners were also taken. Commandos were expected to act swiftly and ruthlessly. They were, by their very nature, fighters dedicated to killing the enemy and preserving their own and their comrades' lives by force of arms.

Of the four 'operations' in which I took part, three were successful. We were compelled to beat a retreat on only one occasion, and by that time all but five of our team had been notionally killed, wounded or taken prisoner. Covered in bruises and cuts, we returned to Dunoon for debriefing with our denim overalls in tatters.

⋆ ⋆ ⋆

For two days, as May, 1942, drew to a close, abnormal activity reigned at our own HQ and in other units. We were issued with warm underclothes, thick sweaters, new denims devoid of insignia, and boots of novel design with moulded rubber soles. These articles had to be stowed away in our kitbags, which bore nothing but our regimental numbers. We were confined to our respective quarters and denied leave. Even the local pubs were declared off-limits. Clearly something was in the wind.

At four o'clock one morning we boarded some tarpaulin-shrouded trucks, chain-smoking to dispel the butterflies in our bellies. A few elements of HQ Group remained behind at Dunoon, which at least seemed to indicate that we were scheduled to return there in due course.

Our destination turned out to be Oban on the Firth of Lorn, where we saw two steamers lying at anchor. We were ferried out to one of them by some landing craft like those familiar to me from my time at Thurso. The ship itself, the

Princesse Elisabeth, formerly a Belgian cross-Channel ferry on the Dover-Ostend run, was equally familiar to me because I had often sailed in her between 1934 and 1936. The other vessel was a French passenger ferry that used to ply between Newhaven and Dieppe. I had noticed at Oban that men of No. 4 Commando were also involved in the operation, but they embarked in the French ship and we didn't see them again.

We were not the only troops on board the *Princesse Elisabeth*. Apart from a few Norwegians whom I had met at Thurso, our fellow passengers included some Canadians and a British light tank unit, but we ourselves were confined to the upper decks and strictly segregated.

We headed out of the Firth of Lorn at nightfall — the French ship having preceded us by several hours — and enjoyed a good night's rest in our hammocks. The sea next day was just as calm, but so foggy that nothing could be seen, though we occasionally heard an aircraft fly overhead. Our officers didn't seem to know where we were bound for — either that, or they kept the information to themselves. That night, although the fog had dispersed, the rhythm of the engines indicated that we were proceeding at slow speed. I had the impression that we were circling.

On the third day sounds of great activity came from the lower decks, where the British tanks were stowed. Then came a rumour that we were returning to port. False alarm: we could tell from the position of the sun that we were still circling.

Most of us were asleep when, at twelve that night, we were roused from our hammocks and told to prepare for a large-scale exercise. We assembled in the ship's dining-room where a blackboard had been set up and maps were projected on a large screen. I gathered from the shape of the islands visible on these maps that we were just off the Hebrides. We were still being briefed on the operation and assigned our objectives when a rattle of chains indicated that the *Princesse Elisabeth* had dropped anchor.

An hour later our instructors set off to occupy the positions which it would be our task to assault and capture. We heard their landing craft splash into the sea. All we could do was wait, playing cards or dozing.

At 2.45 a.m. it was our turn to take our places in the landing craft. There was no moon, smoking had been strictly prohibited and we were ordered to surrender our cigarettes and lighters. Only we commandos seemed to be taking part in the exercise, because no sound issued from the lower decks: the fortunate tank men slept on undisturbed.

Wearing life-jackets, we clambered down the nets that had by now been draped over the ship's side. Our landing craft, commanded and crewed by British and Norwegian naval personnel, headed for the shore. The coastline looked bleak and inhospitable and the jagged rocks whipped the waves into a line of white foam that seemed a portent of the dangers lurking beyond it. Also visible in the gloom were some small, sandy coves that would, in theory, enable us to land in safety.

We had embarked in three landing craft. The one in the centre headed straight for a little beach with ours some distance astern. All at once the darkness was pierced by countless dots of light and we heard the chatter of machine guns. Flares went up, painting the scene a weird shade of grey. We noted that the enemy defences were concentrated at three particular points. This tallied with the 'secret information from the local Resistance' which had been communicated to us on board ship.

Seeing that the first assault craft was enfiladed, we backed off fast and rounded a headland. There, aided by the light of flares but shielded from enemy fire, we sighted another stretch of sand in a small cove whose entrance was guarded by rocks. The landing craft had to go astern to avoid these, leaving us with no choice but to wade ashore. Into the icy water we went, holding our weapons above our heads. Once we were on dry land the automatic responses we had cultivated in training took over. Splitting up into mutually supportive pairs, we outflanked the enemy by sneaking through the rocks and scaling the cliff beyond. Silence was essential at this stage of the operation, so our new rubber-soled boots proved a great asset.

We were strictly forbidden to betray our position by opening fire except in self-defence but authorized to use our commando knives. A lengthy detour along the clifftop enabled us to creep up on the position we had been ordered to neutralize. A few well-aimed thunder-flashes did the job. Although our little team had succeeded in carrying out the first part of its mission, the 'enemy' were now aware of our presence. We finally made it back to the beach, but five of our number were adjudged to have been killed or wounded. The team operating in the centre had been wiped out, the one on the right flank forced to withdraw under heavy enemy fire.

It was 1 p.m. when we rejoined the *Princesse Elisabeth*. Tired out after our exertions, we were welcomed with some liquid refreshment. Our team was congratulated during the debriefing that followed. Our reward after a strenuous operation lasting ten hours — just to remind us that commandos weren't wimps — was an hour's physical jerks!

That evening our ship put in at Stornoway, a small seaport on the Isle of Lewis. We were forbidden to patronize the pubs but allowed to do some shopping. I bought a fine length of genuine tweed which my London tailor converted into a sports jacket so durable that I wore it for many years after the war.

We returned to Dunoon the next day. The true purpose of this operation was never revealed to us, but the presence of the British and Canadian units that did not participate in our exercise suggested that a landing in Norway had been planned but abandoned at short notice. We learned that the French ship had turned back during our second day at sea.

7

Operation Sark

AT the beginning of June, 1942, I was unexpectedly granted some leave and told to change into civvies, take the train to London, and present myself at a hotel near Portman Square.

I was hailed on entering the hotel lounge by a young man built like an international rugby player. He slapped me on the back and addressed me by the name I bore in No. 12 Commando. 'Long time no see, Guy,' he said. 'Let's go and have a bite of lunch.' So he knew my name and what I looked like — he may even have had a photograph of me in his pocket. I was already so inured to surprises that it didn't faze me.

We lunched at one of the more exclusive clubs in Pall Mall, almost opposite the London offices of the Holland America Line, my place of work in 1934. Sharing our table was a major in the Coldstream Guards whom I identified after the War as Ian Collins. We began by conversing on general topics, but I gradually sensed that the others were trying to pump me about my past history, recent and more remote. Entering into the spirit of the game, I spun them the following yarn.

Born in Paris, I was the son of an Englishman who had married a French wife during the 1914 – 18 war. After the war my father had taken a job with the League of Nations in Geneva, where we lived. When he was killed in a car crash my mother returned to her family in Marseilles. I won a scholarship to Harvard, but the outbreak of war prompted me to abandon my studies and sail for England to do my patriotic duty. As for my military career thus far, I said, the other two must be just as well-informed about it as I myself.

This last remark tickled the major's sense of humour and we parted with a firm handshake. I was authorized to visit my friends in London (the parents of Sibyl the WAAF), who were described as 'all right', and told that a car would come to collect me the next morning.

The car, when it turned up, contained the major and two men whom I'd never seen before. We left London and headed in the direction of Brighton — but not, I presumed, for a seaside holiday. The major introduced me to his companions by a new name which was, I'm sure, quite as fictitious as theirs. I never discovered their true identity, though one of them was Scottish, to judge by his unmistakable accent, and their manner towards the major inclined me to think that they were NCOs.

Later, when we were alone together, the major explained the reason for my presence. He told me that my commando training marks were excellent. My tenacity had not gone unnoticed, I could pass for either English or French, and the story I'd concocted over lunch had satisfied him that I wasn't a security risk. I had neatly avoided the trap he'd set me concerning my military activities. The major's verdict on my French fellow commandos was harsh but, in many cases, regrettably accurate: 'We can't entirely trust them. They talk big, they open their mouths too wide, and they're fundamentally indisciplined.'

* * *

The Grange Hotel near Goring-by-Sea, our temporary abode, was occupied by a few elderly couples, the husbands being retired officers who had moved there from London to escape the bombing. They included a Gurkha lieutenant-colonel, an admiral, and another senior officer whose face was largely obscured by an impressive moustache. They were a pleasant, quiet bunch of people, and it seemed obvious that the Grange was an environment in which total security reigned.

The day after our arrival we were joined by another major and a Royal Navy lieutenant. We assembled in the hotel smoking-room, where it was impressed on me, yet again, that absolute secrecy must be preserved both before and after the operation into which I was about to be initiated.

Its objective was Sark, the smallest of the four main Channel Islands forming part of the United Kingdom but currently under German occupation. The enemy had established an E-boat base on Sark and this was proving a thorn in the side of the British system for recovering pilots brought down in the Channel. The authorities were extremely anxious to acquire more detailed information about this base, so our task would be to gather it without drawing attention to ourselves. A rocky island some three miles long, Sark is situated between the two principal islands, Jersey and Guernsey. It had a peacetime population of only five hundred, many of whom had been deported to the Continent. Navigating unobserved in these waters was difficult, but that would be up to the naval officer. We possessed a very detailed map of the island — it even gave the probable position of the E-boat base — so we studied the conformation of the rocky coastline with care, concentrating on our projected landing-place in the north.

Then it was off to Littlehampton, a seaside resort with a small harbour. There, wearing Balaclava helmets and good, thick navy duffle-coats over our denims, we boarded one of the MTBs moored alongside the quay. The trip would take several hours, so there was no point in blackening our hands and faces until just before going ashore by dinghy. Armed only with our Colt 45s and some American tommy-guns, which were far superior to our Stens in fire-power and accuracy, we were fully aware of the risks involved in this operation. Hitler's *Kommandobefehl* No. 228 of 18 October, 1942, bluntly stated that 'commandos must be exterminated to the last man'.

Sark was only 130 miles away, but the MTB could not travel at full speed in open sea, so it was just after midnight, or seven hours later, when the landing took place. Although the dark, moonless night was far from ideal for a reconnaissance operation, maximum invisibility at sea was essential to its success, so we had no choice. We heard little air activity, possibly because top-level instructions had been given to steer clear of the area and avoid alerting the enemy anti-aircraft defences.

The naval officer in command of the MTB informed us that we were nearing our chosen landing-place. We smoked a last cigarette below deck, sank a tot of rum to warm ourselves and 'blacked up'. The MTB stopped engines, the rubber dinghy was launched and a seaman helped us to clamber aboard. The boat would return to the same spot in four hours' time. If we failed to signal, it would try again the following night.

There were four of us in the rubber cockleshell, which was rowed by the two men I'd tagged as British NCOs. As soon as we landed one of them was to conceal the dinghy among the rocks and guard it while the other covered him and our eventual withdrawal from a position at the top of the small cliff overlooking the beach. It would also be his job to signal the MTB when we returned.

The major and I set off into the darkness. Before long a small cottage loomed up ahead. We circled it in silence. All seemed well — no sound, no sign of the enemy — so we tapped on the window. It was a calculated risk, but one we had to take.

An old fisherman, thoroughly alarmed by the sight of the two ghostly figures who had emerged from the gloom and roused him from his slumbers, opened the door to us. I addressed him in English, but it wasn't until I switched to French that he grasped the purpose of our nocturnal intrusion and ushered us inside. He told us that there was a German anti-aircraft emplacement only four hundred yards away. The crew of eight who usually manned it were accommodated in an adjacent barn and would not be relieved until six in the morning. The other enemy troops were stationed on the far side of the island, where the E-boat base was situated. The old man must have had sharp eyes and an excellent memory because he produced a pencil and paper and painstakingly drew us a plan of the site complete in every detail. Reluctant to see us leave, he got his wife to pour us a glass of cider, which we accepted with pleasure. Then, with a *Bonne chance, mes amis*', he turned out the light and opened the door. I never knew his surname, but I remember that his wife addressed him as 'Maurice'. Old

Maurice was yet another of the countless patriotic individuals destined never to figure by name in the annals of the Second World War.

The major and I conferred together. Getting to the other side of the island and back would take time and prevent us from keeping our rendezvous with the MTB. We would have to link up with the other two members of our team, conceal the dinghy more carefully and spend an entire day in hiding without food or water. It would be risky, not only for us but for the crew of the MTB, who would have to come back for us. Having already gleaned so much detailed information from our old fisherman, we decided that the game wasn't worth the candle. We did, however, have enough time left for a close look at the anti-aircraft emplacement. It was a shame we didn't have any explosives, but sabotage was not the purpose of our mission.

Not far away we sighted what looked like a series of large metal boxes mounted on concrete blocks. Though unable to get too close because of barbed wire, we noticed that the cables issuing from them led to a vehicle like one I'd seen while in training, a German command truck captured by the British in Libya. Never having come across such an installation before, we thought it might be useful to memorize the layout and make some notes.

Near the barn we also made out a well-camouflaged hut, and, in the midst of some bushes, a little corrugated iron shed. Music and a babble of voices were coming from the anti-aircraft gunners' quarters. A crack of light appeared as the door opened and shut. Now that the overcast had thinned and our eyes were accustomed to the darkness, we saw a figure making for the little shed — a latrine, as we realized when he entered it and dropped his pants, not troubling to shut the door. Simultaneously seized with the same audacious idea, the major and I exchanged a glance and grinned. The German soldier was unarmed and engrossed in his call of nature, so why not nab him and spirit him back to England?

He didn't hear us sneak up on him as he emerged from the latrine still fumbling with his pants. A commando neck-lock from behind, a gag in his mouth, and it was all over in a flash. Necessity being the mother of invention in such circumstances, we lashed his legs together with his own belt and tied his hands behind his back with a couple of handkerchiefs. The whole incident had passed off without a sound.

The MTB was due back in half an hour, so we decided to head for the dinghy as quickly as possible, taking it in turns to carry our 'package' on our backs. It would be safer to await the boat's arrival at sea: if we lingered ashore for too long the prisoner's comrades might smell a rat and come looking for him. Obliterating any traces of our presence as best we could, we scrambled aboard the dinghy, which was now overloaded and hard to handle. It had started to rain, providentially so, because anyone ashore would find it harder to spot us.

Before long we heard the muffled throb of the MTB's engines as it approached at slow speed. An exchange of signals and we were soon alongside. The crew were more than astonished to see that the dinghy contained five men instead of four, one of them in German uniform.

We conducted a preliminary interrogation during the return trip. Being a German-speaker, I undertook this task. To my surprise, our captive replied in a mixture of German and French, which he spoke with a strong Walloon accent. Clearly delighted to have been taken prisoner, he turned out to be a native of Eupen-Malmédy, a territory annexed to Belgium after the First World War and incorporated in the Third Reich when the Germans invaded it in 1940. He had been conscripted into the Wehrmacht and assigned to an anti-aircraft regiment.

My knowledge of Belgium made it easy for me to verify the prisoner's statements. Very talkative, he was fully acquainted with Sark's defences and the composition of the units stationed on the island. The unfamiliar installation we had seen was a new radar system so secret that he himself had been forbidden to enter the command truck. He had also spent some time in Jersey, so he had plenty to tell us.

We split up when we returned to

Littlehampton, and I never saw the other members of the team again. I retrieved my suitcase from the Grange Hotel and returned to London, where I checked into the small hotel near Portman Square that had now become a familiar haunt of mine.

The officer who had greeted me on my arrival turned up the next day. He asked a lot of questions, requested me to submit a detailed report on the operation and emphasized, yet again, that I was pledged to absolute secrecy until the end of the war.

No need to describe how fully I took advantage of the week's leave in London that followed. I would not, I was told, be returning to Dunoon and No. 12 Commando. My new outfit was to be No. 10 Commando, the interallied unit then in process of formation. The destination on my movement order was Portmadoc, North Wales.

★ ★ ★

In 1946, when I returned to London to conduct certain investigations of which more will be said in due course, I took the opportunity to consult some secret files to which the authorities had granted me access. That was how I learned who had mounted the Sark operation.

COHQ (Combined Operations HQ) and the SOE (Special Operations Executive) had jointly set up the SSRF (Small Scale Raiding Force), subsequently known as No. 63 Commando. I thought it probable that the major and the two British NCOs belonged to that unit, the existence of which was a carefully guarded secret. I further surmised, from its 'Top Secret' classification, that the unit was still active, possibly in Palestine or elsewhere.

8

No. 10 (Interallied) Commando

ACCORDING to the historians who have written numerous books about it, No. 10 Commando was one of the most extraordinary military formations that has ever come into being. On 7 January, 1943, the *News Chronicle* described it as 'something of an experiment embarked upon with some trepidation, for it involved the creation of an unknown quantity, bringing together men of all nationalities with, in some cases, conflicting points of view.'

Lord Mountbatten had long believed that advantage should be taken of the local knowledge and languages of those who had recently fled their homes on the European mainland. With the exception of the Pioneer Corps, which was not, strictly speaking, a combatant formation, United Kingdom corps and regiments did not admit foreigners to their ranks, so

104

some means had to be found of utilizing this potentially valuable asset.

In 1941, after reading reports of commando raids on Norway's Lofoten Islands, the French naval lieutenant P. Kieffer built up a nucleus of similar units at 'Surcouf', the Free French Navy's headquarters on Clapham Common. Born in Haiti, Kieffer had worked in the United States before the outbreak of war and had then returned to France to enlist in the navy as a volunteer. When Dunkirk fell he was sent to England and posted to the *Amiral Courbet*, an old French cruiser berthed at Portsmouth. Shooting down the occasional enemy aircraft was all that ever broke the monotony of life on board and Kieffer itched for a more belligerent role.

The French military authorities in London evinced little enthusiasm for his idea, so he approached the British instead. His sole French sponsor, Admiral Muselier, was unable to provide the necessary funds or equipment but arranged a meeting with Brigadier J. C. Haydon, who then commanded the Special Service Brigade. Two weeks later, Kieffer enrolled his first volunteers: Quartier-Maître (Leading Seaman) Francis Vourch and sixteen other ratings, of whom five had just been released from detention. Such was the peculiar little outfit that presented itself for training at Achnacarry and was soon afterwards designated the *1ère Compagnie de Fusiliers Marins Commandos*. Wearing hexagonal insignia adorned with the Croix de Lorraine and the blue beret and red pompon of the Marine Nationale, its members were incorporated into No. 4 Commando and stationed at Ayr in Scotland.

The idea of forming an international commando made up of men from various countries slowly but steadily gained favour. On 26 June, 1942, Lieutenant-Colonel Dudley Lister, then commanding No. 4 Commando, attended a meeting of the Establishment Committee at the War Ministry in London. No. 10 Commando came into being on 2 July, less than a week later, and Lister was appointed its first commanding officer.

The various national elements were stationed in North Wales. On 14 July, 1942, No. 1 Troop (French) installed itself at Criccieth, No. 2 Troop (Dutch) at Portmadoc, and HQ Troop (British) at Harlech. They were followed by No. 4 Troop (Belgian), No. 5 Troop (Norwegian), and No. 6 Troop (Polish), which were based, respectively, at Abersoch, Nefyn and Caernarvon.

Another extremely mysterious unit, designated 'X Troop', made its appearance near Aberdovey. This consisted of Austrians, Czechs, Yugoslavs, Hungarians and even Germans, all of whom had been given English names and issued with British Army paybooks.

The commandos' official club at Harlech was called 'The Melting-Pot', appropriately enough, and it was there that all these nationalities mingled on occasion.

★ ★ ★

Thus it was that I bade farewell to London yet again, leaving behind some very pleasant memories and — immodest of me though it may be to say so — a few tears occasioned by my renewed disappearance. Girls can become rather sentimental in wartime.

Crewe Junction at dead of night was hardly the most congenial place to spend an hour changing trains for North Wales, but at least I had time to console myself with a mug of hot tea at the NAAFI canteen on the platform. (Incidental note: it has always been a mystery to me how the English manage to brew decent tea in five-gallon urns!)

I found myself a comfortable, well-upholstered corner seat and settled down to sleep. Like a little dog cocking its leg against every lamp post, the train stopped innumerable times. After a circuitous journey by way of Caernarvon, site of the ancient castle founded by Edward I seven hundred years earlier, the train finally pulled into Portmadoc station. My movement order stated that I must report to the headquarters of No. 2 Troop, 10 Commando, which was housed in the little station of the narrow-gauge railway linking Portmadoc with Blaenau Ffestiniog, currently out of service. I made my way there down the long village street, but the building was locked and deserted — not a trace of military activity to be seen.

Having noticed a police station while walking down the street, I retraced my steps. 'Yes, we're expecting a new intake any time now,' I was told by the stout, mustachioed constable enthroned behind the desk. 'An officer warned us to expect one, but that's all we know. Try Major Andrews, the local Home Guard commander. He may have some more information.' In addition to being the proprietor and manager of a slate quarry in the mountains, Major Andrews owned the narrow-gauge railway and the station that was supposed to be our headquarters. Another constable showed me the way to his house near the little harbour at the end of the main street.

Andrews, a charming man, told me that two officers, one English and one Dutch, had called on him to arrange billets for their men, who were scheduled to arrive early that afternoon. His wife invited me to have lunch *en famille* and wait for them in the drawing-room. It was a pleasant introduction to my time at Portmadoc.

The first group to arrive included a number of familiar figures, one of them being my old friend John Steengracht. Our troop commander, Captain P. J. Mulder, was assisted by Lieutenants Maarten Knottenbelt, Jan Linzel and Ruysch van Dugteren. Knottenbelt, who spoke perfect English, had been brought up in England and was reading for a degree at Oxford when war broke out. Van Dugteren had come to England from South Africa, and Linzel's escape from Holland had entailed braving the perils of the North Sea in a small boat.

The whole intake found billets by nightfall. John and I, who had teamed up again, were allocated one of the best, a spacious bed-sitter in a house in the main street near our headquarters. We took it on the recommendation of Major Andrews, who knew the owners well.

★ ★ ★

The first task that devolved on us was to renovate the little station prior to setting up our headquarters there. Armed with hammers, nails, pots of paint and sacks of plaster and cement, we were severely tested in the role of carpenters, bricklayers and decorators. The result was a triumph and the premises became a jewel in No. 10 Commando's crown.

Promoted instructor and awarded my first stripes, I was sent on a number of supplementary courses. The first of these, a security course, took me to an Edinburgh suburb. There, in addition to the security measures to be implemented in any hush-hush unit, I was schooled in many other aspects of security. The examination I had to sit after twelve days of concentrated study covered a wide variety of topics including the identification of enemy equipment and aircraft, the structure and organization of German and Italian land, sea and air forces, and their badges of rank and insignia. This and the other courses I attended were not only extremely interesting but proved of great value to me later on, when I found myself in occupied territory. By the time I completed them my notes filled no less than seven exercise books.

On returning to Portmadoc, I was appointed 'security officer' of No. 2 Troop, 10 Commando — rather a high-flown title for a humble corporal. After attending two more courses, one devoted to sabotage and the other to camouflage, I felt like a fully-fledged commando and ready for action.

In order to carry out a preliminary selection and weed out any unsuitable candidates, the intakes we received were subjected to ten days' training at Achnacarry. It was our job, as instructors, to transform these recruits into genuine fighting soldiers — no picnic, because we had to maintain our supposedly superior status by outdoing them at everything. Many were the times when I had to carry, in addition to my own tommy-gun, the 2-inch mortar or Bren of a 'new boy' who couldn't make the grade.

As time went by, our field exercises and night marches became longer and more arduous. The favourite locations for these were Harlech's long sandy beach and the countryside around Snowdon, which rises to a height of 3,500 feet. We often held exercises in conjunction with the commando's other troops. Of these the French proved the wiliest nocturnal adversaries and the Poles the roughest and toughest.

Our most arduous exercise entailed a forced march of 80 kilometres to Holyhead at the tip of the island of Anglesey. Following us uphill and down dale were some supply trucks, a mobile canteen, and — to pick up any exhausted stragglers who fell by the wayside — an ambulance. Anglesey is separated from the mainland by the Menai Strait, which is spanned by an iron railway bridge several hundred yards long. This we had to traverse by way of the girders, first having silently 'neutralized' the guards posted there. Of the seventy men who embarked on this exercise, only about thirty completed it.

For the cause which lacks assistance,
For the wrong which needs resistance,
For the future in the distance,
And the good that I can do!

Such was the motto of No. 2 Troop, 10 (Interallied) Commando, and such was the spirit that prevailed within our ranks. In contrast to the military class system

113

customary in those days, officers and men rubbed shoulders in an unconstrained, comradely manner. The respect we felt for our superiors stemmed from the example they set, not from the pips or stripes that adorned their battledress, though this didn't deter us from playing an occasional practical joke on them.

Maarten Knottenbelt, who had once been a scoutmaster and thought he knew all there was to know about orienteering, was a compass 'freak'. One night, when he was leading a party through the mountains, we played a dirty trick on him. We doctored one of the unit's compasses, which were all identical, by carefully concealing a tiny magnet in its base. This caused the needle to deviate from magnetic north by some twenty degrees. Maarten had a habit of leaving his things lying around, so it was child's play to substitute the doctored compass for his own.

Divided up into two teams and dropped at different points, we were instructed to rendezvous at a particular map reference. One team was headed by Maarten, sole possessor of a compass and confident of his ability to use it; the other, to which I myself belonged, was led by a sergeant. I had a good bump of direction, having spent my boyhood in the mountains, and map-reading held no mysteries for me. The sergeant, who was in the know, had complete faith in me, especially as I had gone shooting over the same ground with John Steengracht and Major Andrews.

We reached the rendezvous. One hour went by, then another. Finally the second team appeared, looking haggard and exhausted. They had lost their way in the mountains, thanks to the doctored compass, and it was all we could do to conceal our mirth at Maarten's discomfiture. We convinced him that his pet gadget had gone haywire because of some ferrous rocks below ground. He never discovered the truth, so he tended to boast less often of his expert fieldcraft.

★ ★ ★

John and I were on excellent terms with Major Andrews. He often invited us to eat at his home, where Mrs

Andrews produced some delicious off-ration dinners of wild duck and venison, a rare treat in wartime. He also invited us to join his shooting parties. The land he owned included some 250 acres of marshy ground in the little delta formed by the Glaslyn before it flows into Tremadoc Bay. This area, Traeth Mawr by name, was a hunter's paradise inhabited by countless wild duck and wading birds.

Andrews lent me and John (an inveterate hunter of human 'birds' as well) two fine shotguns and authorized us to practise our skill with them. We used to rise before dawn and pedal off to Traeth Mawr on bicycles 'borrowed' from the army, and we seldom returned empty-handed. The only trouble was that we possessed no dogs, so we had to retrieve our birds wearing boots unsuited to the marshy ground. Despite this, morning roll call found us punctually on parade outside Troop HQ, washed, shaved and smartly turned out. Our officers, who knew that we had the major's blessing, shut their eyes to these early morning excursions.

★ ★ ★

Portmadoc church was situated in the main street and we often cast covetous eyes at its tower and the clock whose chimes formed a regular accompaniment to our days and nights.

There were four of us in the club when the challenge was issued: were we, as 'old commandos', capable of scaling the tower? It was eleven p.m. Memories of our assault on the water-tower at Stratford revived as we hurried back to our billets before lights-out to fetch our toggle ropes and don our denims and rubber-soled boots.

Hugging the walls to avoid a brush with the military police patrol that prowled Portmadoc at this hour, we assembled in the little garden behind the church. We had previously discovered that the wall on that side might be easier to scale because it displayed more projections. The gutter might provide an anchorage for our toggle ropes, but would it be strong enough? Being the lightest member of the party, I led off. Our troubles were far from over when we had scaled the wall, because the slate roof was very steep and too smooth to afford any purchase. We had no ladder, so I managed to gain the ridge beside the church tower by using the others' prone bodies as a human ladder. Before long the four of us were seated astride the ridge with the clock some twelve or thirteen feet above us.

To reach it we employed the same acrobatic technique as before. As the lightest, I was the last to go. It was like mountaineering without a rope, and any slip might have been fatal from my point of view. At last I found something to hang on to: the face of the clock itself. I secured myself to it by attaching my toggle rope to a convenient bolt. It was nearly 1 a.m. by now and the clock had been deafening us with its chimes every quarter of an hour. Although the cogs were very stiff, I managed to wrench the hour hand round until it said two o'clock instead of one. We had attained our objective.

Abseiling down was far easier than climbing up, but delayed reaction set in once we were back on the ground. We rested for a minute or two and smoked a surreptitious cigarette to steady our nerves, not to mention our hands, which were trembling like aspen leaves. Then we slunk back to our billets.

It wasn't until the next afternoon that someone informed the vicar that his clock was an hour fast. Having no sense of humour, he was furious. He immediately — and correctly — inferred from the imprints of our boots in his trampled flower beds that the perpetrators of this misdeed were rascally commandos. On the additional grounds that we had dislodged some stones and damaged his slate roof, he reported the matter to the police, who launched an inquiry.

Our CO had enough on his plate without having to worry about legal proceedings that might have earned him a black mark. Knowing in any case that the secret could not be kept for long, we went to his office and owned up. The outcome of the affair was a week's confinement to barracks and the loss of our next spell of leave. The other members of the troop, who were waiting when we emerged from headquarters, bore us in triumph down the main street. The local inhabitants applauded, and even the three policemen joined the procession. As for the cost of repairs to the church, this was met by a whip-round among our fellow commandos.

It was no fun losing a spell of leave, of course, especially as that punishment went hand in hand with fatigues from which we, as instructors, were normally exempted. No welcome break in the monotony of camp life for us. Those were the days when the voice of Vera Lynn, 'the forces' sweetheart', dominated the airwaves. In our present, leave-starved condition, the words of one particular lyric made us feel more than usually wistful:

> I haven't said thanks for that lovely week-end,
> those few days in heaven you helped me to spend . . .

★ ★ ★

From time to time, No. 2 Troop had to do guard duty at 10 Commando headquarters in Harlech. Our CO, Dudley

Lister, made a habit of attending guard mounting whenever he was at HQ, but he was notorious for his unpunctuality. This besetting sin had already caused a rumpus on a previous occasion, when the French troop had simply walked off and left the Norwegians to take over without performing the traditional ceremony. We decided to adopt a different and more humorous procedure.

Predictably Lister was too late to see us take over from our Polish comrades, who speedily returned to their quarters in Caernarvon. Having procured a dozen cardboard dummies of the kind we used for target practice, we dressed them up in uniform and put them in the Poles' place. The CO's face was a picture when he finally showed up, but he took the joke in good part and commanded the dummies to stand at ease.

★ ★ ★

Another memory of this period comes to mind. The ruins of Harlech Castle were only a stone's throw from 10 Commando HQ and we delighted in scaling them at night. This did not please the local Home Guard, who regarded the castle grounds as their own domain and held exercises there. One night we decided to take some prisoners, march them back to headquarters and shut them up in the guardroom. Rousing the orderly officer, we maintained that we had spotted them prowling around our post and captured them on suspicion of being spies. The Home Guardsmen didn't appreciate the joke, and I don't think they ever forgave us.

★ ★ ★

Christmas, 1942, came and went, 1943 dawned. We were awarded our green berets and wore them with pride, but I was growing tired of doing nothing more active than training recruits. There was a limit to the number of practical jokes we could devise and the pleasure we derived from putting them into effect.

At long last I received an order that made my heart pound with impatience: I was to leave Portmadoc and return to London.

9

Agent Training

I WAS back in London, this time in commando uniform. My initial excitement had subsided a little. Being accustomed to security precautions, I was puzzled that my movement order clearly stated the address to which I had to report. This lack of secrecy caused me to doubt if anything of great importance awaited me there.

I made my way to Park Street, Mayfair, climbed four flights of stairs, rang the bell of the relevant apartment and was conducted to a pantry off the kitchen. The general impression was shambolic: papers littered the floor, shelves were stacked with files, copies of orders, telegrams and other documents. Having introduced themselves, two Dutch officers, Marine Colonel M. R. de Bruyne and Lieutenant-Commander Lieftinck, asked me point-blank if I would like to attend a series of courses with a view to infiltrating German-occupied territory and using the knowledge I had gained to assist members of the Resistance.

I accepted their offer on the spot. At this stage in the brief interview a British officer made his appearance. He was introduced to me as Major Blunt, though I later discovered that his real name was Bingham.

The other three asked me to wait before launching into a discussion of subjects that should not, in the normal course of events, have been aired in my presence. Then, suddenly remembering that I was still in the room, they told me to come back the next day. Sensitized by my prior training, I was astonished at their amateurism and neglect of elementary security measures — so astonished that I wondered if they were deliberately testing my discretion.

No accommodation had been provided for me, so I begged a bed from Sibyl's parents, the Stibbings, who lived near by. I was outside the Park Street flat on the dot next morning, but it was half an hour before a secretary turned up. She informed me that Major Blunt was expecting me at an address in Baker Street. I already knew the building in question, having visited it during the Sark operation, and was happy to find myself back on familiar territory.

No. 82 Baker Street, known to outsiders as St Michael's House, Marks & Spencer's administrative offices, had a rear entrance in the mews that ran behind it. To lessen the risk that their comings and goings might attract unwelcome attention, this was the entrance customarily employed by SOE personnel.

A long, dark passage led straight to the old-fashioned lift that gave access to the floors above. I went up to a waiting-room where everyone coming or going was closely scrutinized by a commissionaire who ensured that all who entered or left the premises had a clean bill of health. A blonde in ATS uniform preceded me along a maze of corridors, giving me plenty of time to admire her immaculate figure and the perfect contours of her slender legs. Whether or not she sensed my appreciative gaze, she favoured me with a half-smile. No doubt about it, today had begun far more promisingly than the day before.

With its big Georgian table and capacious leather armchairs, the room into which I was shown resembled the smoking-room of an exclusive London club. Comfortably ensconced there with a glass of sherry at his elbow, Major Blunt was talking to a man in civilian clothes. The latter proved to be Lieutenant-Commander Holmes, RNVR, who, in keeping with his name and Baker Street sphere of operations, was one of the SOE sleuths who helped to assess candidates for membership of the organization.

I was released from my oath of secrecy and instructed to present a minutely detailed account of my civilian and military career to date. I was also asked a number of trick questions. My only respite from this friendly but searching interrogation, which lasted all day long, occurred when we broke for a light lunch served by the eye-catching ATS girl.

By nightfall I was feeling worn out but happy. This was the real thing at last: I had been accepted for agent training. I was driven to the now familiar hotel near

Portman Square and informed that a car would pick me up next morning.

★ ★ ★

Another pretty face awaited me when I emerged from the hotel: a girl driver in the smart uniform of the FANY, or First Aid Nursing Yeomanry. We headed south-west, drove through Guildford and entered the grounds of a large, secluded private house.

My first STS (Special Training School) proved to be Wanborough Manor, a 14th-century house owned by the earl of Onslow but currently at the disposal of the SOE. This was where many agents underwent their primary training in an atmosphere that had little in common with military routine. I soon realized that Wanborough was an establishment devoted to the testing and observation of candidates' reactions.

In the bar, which was open all day, prospective agents who had drunk too deeply were coaxed by FANY participants in the 'game' into revealing details of their previous history. Not unnaturally, this sometimes bred relationships of undue intimacy, and it was not uncommon for a candidate to be whisked off overnight to some camp in Scotland for subsequent reassignment to his unit or some other branch of the Service. I heard later that this form of psychological test had been abandoned because it resulted in too much wastage, not only among would-be agents but also among the young female volunteers, whose feelings of love or compassion dissuaded them from playing the game any longer.

The courses at Wanborough were theoretical. How to become a poised, competent agent capable of weighing up a course of action before embarking on it, how to react under severe and prolonged interrogation, how to acquire the sixth sense that would alert one to the presence of a 'tail', how to avoid traps — such were the main subjects we covered, and the knowledge we acquired was put into practice at a later stage.

★ ★ ★

I was exempted from a visit to the STS at Lochailort in Scotland, having already completed my commando training, so the next hurdle that confronted me was a parachute training course. A small party of us were met at Manchester station by a mustachioed sergeant and escorted to Altrincham, where we were installed in a secluded house.

The Airborne Troops Parachute School was situated at Tatton Park, on the edge of Ringway aerodrome, which now forms part of Manchester Airport. This was where nearly all British Army paratroops carried out their preliminary jumps. Tacked on to an intake already in training, we were taken to the big hangar at Ringway for a crash course in how to roll over on hitting the ground, how to haul on the shroud lines so as to change direction or modify our rate of descent and thereby avoid landing in trees or colliding with obstacles, how to position ourselves in relation to the wind so as not to land on our backs, how to bundle up a parachute and release the harness in double-quick time rather than be dragged along the ground. Muscular arms and supple legs were essential to a good landing in the days when parachutes took only nine seconds to fall the last fifty metres. They have become considerably more sophisticated since then!

Having joined the course half-way through, we were sentenced to jump the very next day. No practice jumps from the tower or balloon for us, even though we had twiddled our thumbs for three whole days prior to our departure for Manchester — yet another weird and wonderful example of military co-ordination.

With parachutes firmly strapped to our backs, I and five other novices boarded the old Whitley bomber that awaited us at the end of the runway. The ripcords or 'static lines' that would open our chutes were secured to the interior of the fuselage, the door was closed, the aircraft lumbered along the runway and took off with a deafening roar that hurt our eardrums. The Whitley, of course, had none of the sound-proofing or pressurization that enables passengers in a modern airliner to travel in comfort.

The dispatcher opened the lid over the

circular hole in the floor through which we were to make our exit. I don't suffer from vertigo, so I felt no fear, just a slight tingling sensation in the pit of my stomach.

The first to jump, I perched on the edge of the hole with my legs dangling in space and my eyes fixed on the luminous telltales. The red light was still on.

The red light went out, the green came on, the despatcher yelled 'Go!' Legs clamped together and arms at my sides, I launched myself into space. Buffeted by the Whitley's slipstream, I saw its tail disappear from view above me. Then, with a sudden jerk, the ripcord did its job and my chute snapped open.

I was overcome by a feeling of calm, of total detachment from the things of this world, as I floated earthwards with the wind whispering in the silken canopy overhead. The view was magnificent, but I didn't have long to appreciate it. Now was the time to apply the principles I'd learned by rote. I kept my legs clamped together so as not to let them catch the wind and make me spin like a top, turning my chute into a deadly 'streamer'. Then, having relaxed them during the last few feet of the descent. I landed, rolled over on one shoulder, got up quickly and unbuckled by harness. Hauling on the lower shroud lines to prevent the wind from ballooning the chute, I bundled it up and doubled to the assembly point, where our instructors had been watching with pencils poised over clipboards.

My first jump was a success. I hadn't even heard the sergeant's megaphoned instructions, but it didn't matter, I scored seventeen out of twenty. The next man to land hit the ground with his legs apart and got bawled out for his pains.

I did another two jumps that day and three more the next, one of them in darkness. That completed the course. I was now entitled to wear the winged chute on my chest, the coveted insignia of a qualified parachutist.

★ ★ ★

After Ringway came three more STS courses, each of which entailed assimilating a vast amount of information. It was a hard slog and far more taxing than my most onerous days at the Harvard Business School.

My next port of call was STS No. 17 at Hatfield, in Hertfordshire, where we were instructed in radiotelegraphy, the encoding of messages, and the rudiments of industrial sabotage. The last subject was taught in a purely theoretical manner, but my commando training had already given me a practical grounding in the identification of sabotage objectives and the use of explosives, including limpets and magnetic charges. Although I was not to be trained as a wireless operator, I had to become familiar with the basic procedures. Codes, of which I would often have to make use, were my principal focus of interest.

From Hatfield I was sent for additional training to a small manor house at Tempsford in Bedfordshire, one of the numerous airfields that dotted the English countryside in those days. Security was strict there, but I noticed that one of the huts was marked 'No. 161 Squadron Officers' Canteen'. Concealed among the trees bordering the airfield were a number of Halifaxes and some smaller aircraft which I took to be reconnaissance planes. These Westland Lysanders and Lockheed Hudsons were, in fact, used for nocturnal operations in enemy-occupied territory. The commandant of the school, an officer in the Fleet Air Arm, introduced us to Hugh Verity, whose Lysander made no less than twenty-two clandestine landings in France during 1943.

Sandwiched between the A1 and the main railway line from London to the north, Tempsford was well camouflaged but only a few miles from Bedford, so the Luftwaffe's persistent failure to raid it was surprising. Nearly forty bombers were based there in 1943. Although the Halifax pilots of 161 and 138 Squadrons took part in conventional bombing raids, they were specially trained to locate the landing sites where their passengers, packages and containers had to be dropped, by visual navigation.

One of our first tasks was to familiarize ourselves with the containers. These were metal cylinders 35 centimetres in diameter and 1.65 metres long. Weighing about 100 kilograms when loaded, they opened longitudinally and could easily be carried by four men using the built-in handles provided. A Halifax, which could accommodate fifteen such containers in its bomb bay, dropped them in sticks, like bombs. As for the packages in the fuselage, the dispatcher simply jettisoned these through the hole in the floor of the plane.

The helicopters of the time were too slow and noisy to be used for operations in enemy territory. Their present-day function was fulfilled by the Lysander, a small, sturdy, high-winged monoplane normally employed by the Army for missions involving co-ordination and observation. Its armament and bomb racks were removed, and a light ladder was secured to the starboard side of the fuselage on a level with the second cockpit usually occupied by the navigator-observer.

The Lysander's only crew when in service with 161 Squadron was the pilot, who doubled as his own navigator. Armed only with a large-calibre pistol, he flew the aircraft seated alone in the forward cockpit. The rear cockpit, which was separated from him by a bulkhead, could easily accommodate two passengers, though three or even four were sometimes carried in an emergency. The single-engined plane had a wingspan of 12.71 metres, a cruising speed of 264 k.p.h., a maximum speed of approximately 340 k.p.h., and a maximum range of 1100 kilometres. All it required in the way of a landing strip was 400 metres of flat, grassy terrain.

The course at Tempsford schooled us in the theory and practice of landing-site selection, ground-to-air signalling, and the organization of 'reception committees'. In 1943, apart from visual signals, there existed various top secret methods of communicating with aircraft from England. The most elaborate system, undoubtedly, was the Rebecca/Eureka combination, the most practical the S-Phone. The Lysander was too small to be fitted with Rebecca's long, nine-metre antenna, which was capable of picking up directional beams emitted from the ground by Eureka. Too heavy and cumbersome for the members of a reception committee to carry around with ease, Eureka had an antenna 1.5 metres long mounted on a tripod more than 2 metres high. A dial on board the aircraft indicated its direction and distance from the transmitter. This system could only be used in special circumstances, for instance for set-piece landings by MTBs or larger aircraft like the Hudson, because batteries were quickly exhausted by the amount of electricity it consumed (at least eight watts).

The S-Phone had many advantages. The precursor of the walkie-talkie, it weighed just under seven kilograms and was thoroughly portable. Not only could its signals be picked up 40 kilometres away by an aircraft flying at 3000 metres, but they were hard for the enemy to intercept at ground level — an additional advantage from the security angle. Voices were recognizable and prearranged passwords could be exchanged.

I still retain the greatest admiration for the intrepid pilots and instructors who, after training us all day long, joined us in the bar for a convivial round of drinks, or, if duty called, flew off into the night.

★ ★ ★

My last 'school', though not my final test, took me to Beaulieu in the New Forest, north of Southampton, family seat of the Barons Montagu of Beaulieu. Today the building where we underwent our theoretical training houses the National Motor Museum.

Nestling among the trees not far from the ruined abbey were some attractive chalets containing several bedrooms, a sitting room, a bathroom and a small kitchen. These were where we lived, discreetly guarded by military policemen and looked after by the ATS orderlies who took care of the housework. We ate our meals in the main building but were forbidden to venture more than a certain distance into the grounds.

From my point of view Beaulieu not only recapitulated the many courses I had already attended but tested me on the knowledge I had acquired and enabled me to put it into practice. As prospective agents we were expected to withstand prolonged and drastic interrogations at dead of night, to don civilian clothes and tail or be tailed through the streets of Southampton, to pass messages unobserved, to make clandestine contacts, to conceal documents — in short to learn all the tricks of a trade in which inconspicuousness is the prime requirement.

One of the most interesting aspects of the course, and one that proved useful to me in the field, was the psychological assessment of candidates for recruitment into a network. I also learned enough about burglary and safe-cracking to have made me an expert crook.

★ ★ ★

Of the seventeen candidates for 'network organizer' status, twelve failed their final examinations and were destined to become wireless operators or be transferred to other branches of the Service. Many of them remained on the waiting list for a long time before being assigned to the Jedburgh or SAS teams sent to cooperate with Resistance groups in occupied Europe in support of forthcoming military operations and to instruct them in the use of the weapons dropped to them by parachute. As one of the five successful candidates, I rounded off my Beaulieu episode with a practical exercise in Liverpool.

My task during this exercise, which lasted twelve days, was to go underground in a big English city and carry out a specific mission undetected. My sole link with SOE was a telephone number to be used only in the last resort, for instance if I was arrested by the police or one of the counter-espionage services.

I and my fellow finalists were allowed to choose our own cover stories and provided with false papers to back them up, together with two hundred pounds in cash. Any disbursements from this — to us, astronomical — sum had to be justified after the event.

The object of my mission was to get to the Irish Republic by clandestine and illicit means. The only other information given me was the name and favourite haunt of a person suspected of pro-German activities. Although this was little enough to go on, I would have to get by on my own.

A military uniform being the least conspicuous form of disguise available, that was the one I chose. I wore the insignia of the Pioneer Corps, which, apart from the Commandos, was the only British Army formation to admit foreign volunteers and ex-prisoners of war desirous of serving with the Allies.

My cover story, which seemed devoid of any obvious flaws, was as follows. A native of the Sudetenland, the Czechoslavakian territories inhabited by ethnic Germans, I had been conscripted into the Wehrmacht, captured near El Alamein and shipped back to a PoW camp in England. Once there, I had used my Czech nationality to get me into the Pioneer Corps. Weary of the depressing atmosphere prevailing in that outfit, I had taken advantage of a spell of leave to go AWOL in the hope of getting to neutral Eire, which was reputed to be a paradise for deserters. In addition to photographs of relatives and an imaginary fiancée in the Sudetenland, my false papers included an authentic-looking but out-of-date leave pass.

On arrival in Liverpool I made for a

seedy district near the waterfront and had no difficulty in finding a bed-and-breakfast establishment within easy reach of the pub frequented by the person I was supposed to contact.

Look, listen, and do just enough to get yourself noticed by those whom you hope to entrap: such is the prelude to all operations of this nature. By day I aimlessly roamed the streets until opening time, then made my way to the pub. There, leaning on the bar, I would listen to people chatting and join in the conversation speaking English with a strong German accent. Thanks to this and my Pioneer Corps insignia, I was soon classified as a 'foreigner'. Loosening my tongue by degrees, I expressed covert admiration for the Irish, who had chosen to remain neutral, and for the IRA, whose pro-German sentiments were common knowledge.

I had been given a description of my suspect, Fiona, who taught at a school in the suburb of Everton. A woman of about thirty with an oval face, dark hair gathered on her neck, and magnificent blue eyes, she was easy

142

enough to recognize.

Three evenings went by before I accosted her, a natural enough thing to do in a crowded public bar. Fiona did not seem averse to my company, so I invited her to come to the pictures. She shared her digs with a boy-friend, she told me, but he would be away for some time. I knew from my briefing in London that he was suspected of sabotage and had done a bunk, almost certainly to Ireland.

The fifth day was decisive. Another film show, during which our fingers met and entwined in the darkness, a visit to a dance hall, and I walked her home. After we had kissed and cuddled awhile outside the house where she lived, she asked me in for 'a last cup of tea'.

Bed is by far the best place for exchanging confidences. Impressed by my story, Fiona warned me not to show my face too often in the pub because she suspected that it was under surveillance. Then she promised to help me escape from England.

Next day I moved into a room in the same house, not that I ever used it at night — Fiona's bed and her physical charms were far more appealing. The fish had taken the bait. From now on reading in my room was my sole form of activity during daylight hours.

The tenth day came and still nothing happened. All this waiting in idleness was getting on my nerves. If I didn't pull it off in the next two days I would have to return to London. Then fortune smiled on me: Fiona announced that some friends of hers would sneak me aboard a coaster bound for Cork. When? In two days' time — in other words, on the day my mission was due to end.

That presented a problem: I would have to warn London that I was on the verge of success. I went for a walk, making sure I wasn't followed. 'They' were no fools and they might be suspicious. No one was tailing me, so I made for a telephone box and dialled the Welbeck number I'd memorized. 'Act normally, it'll be all right,' was the response to my unexpected news. I was asked for my present address and told that I would be kept under surveillance. If the worst came to the worst I would wind up in Cork!

Fiona gave me some civilian clothes, a seaman's outfit to be worn when 'they' came to collect me. Our last night together was an energetic affair. Fiona was a passionate young woman and we didn't get much sleep.

Next morning a man in a merchant seaman's peaked cap rang the doorbell, armed with a duffle-bag for me to carry on my shoulder. Our destination was Birkenhead, on the other side of the Mersey estuary. After a brief wait in a warehouse — the coast was clear, or so it seemed — my companion and I headed for the coaster. All hell broke loose just as we reached the foot of the gangway, where we were surrounded by a squad of plainclothesmen who looked to me like Special Branch. An unmarked patrol car drove us to a police station in Liverpool where I found Fiona waiting in handcuffs.

When my own handcuffs were removed on the orders of the senior plainclothesman who had supervised our arrest, she glared at me and spat in my face. Her language, which had ceased to be that of a schoolteacher, might have issued from the lips of an infuriated prostitute and her lovely blue eyes shone with hatred.

I wasn't exactly proud of having hoodwinked her, but such are the hazards — and perks — of the agent's profession. Fiona and her confederates ended the war in a prison camp on the Isle of Man.

* * *

Although it did not form part of an agent's normal training, I underwent a medical experiment which the SOE authorities followed with great interest.

What most concerned me as a future agent was my fear of revealing, under prolonged interrogation or torture, facts that could lead to the arrest of members of my network, thereby destroying it and frustrating all our efforts.

The Stibbings, whom I had known before the war and often stayed with while on leave in London, were friends of Sir Charles Hambro, 'boss' of the SOE. The family had top security clearance, so I was authorized to visit them during my training as a secret agent.

Among the regular visitors to their handsome house near Lancaster Gate was an eminent Harley Street neurologist who knew and greatly respected my father, having attended various lectures of his at London and Edinburgh Universities. While chatting with him one day I confided my fear of cracking under duress. He reassured me. There was a method of preventing this, he said, although in the case of certain individuals it presented a risk that their memory might be permanently impaired. I could try it if I liked, but only with Sir Charles's permission.

The purpose of this peculiar form of therapy, if such it can be termed, is to induce temporary amnesia by autosuggestive means. The subject's volition is indispensable to the method's success because its results must be obtained without any outside assistance. The key to the system is the deliberate creation of a blank in the subject's mind and the superimposition of fiction on fact, for example:

The fact: I met Alphonse at a football

match on Sunday. He informed me that an air drop was expected at X during the night of Tuesday next.

The things to efface from my memory are Alphonse and the information he gave me. It's perfectly all right for me to have attended the football match in question, but I must replace Alphonse with someone else, for instance an imaginary girl, complete with details of how she was dressed, how old she was, her figure, the colour of her eyes and hair, and so on.

So I banish Alphonse from my mind and substitute a girl named Jeanne. She had blue eyes, a snub nose, fair hair, a grey raincoat and a funny little hat. (Here, because the same questions may be asked more than once in the course of the same interrogation, the key to consistency is to use the first name and personal particulars of someone you have known in the past.)

Having blotted out the recollection of what Alphonse told me about the air drop, I substitute the following, carefully memorized story:

I was so taken with Jeanne's pretty

face that I offered her a cigarette and we got into conversation. What did we talk about? Her enthusiasm for the local football team and our respective jobs. She told me she was a hairdresser and I described my job as an insurance inspector, which is full of variety and involves me in a lot of travelling. I asked her to come to the cinema with me, but she refused.

This fiction, which is now firmly rooted in my mind, cannot be dislodged or broken by my interrogators unless they gain access to my unconscious with the aid of certain drugs.

Though mentally taxing, the above method would have saved the lives of many agents who were captured by the Abwehr or Gestapo. I myself used it — and survived.

10

Farewell to London

IN Lancaster Gate, just north of Hyde Park, was a big block of flats, one floor of which had been taken over by SOE as a kind of parking lot for agents waiting to leave for the Continent.

I was back in my old commando uniform, this time adorned with a parachutist's wings and a sergeant's stripes. Although I was entirely free to move around London, I soon spotted that all my doings were under surveillance. If I had had any doubts of this, they were dispelled by the fact that, as soon as I entered a pub, I was buttonholed by a FANY and neutralized for the evening.

On one occasion, when I asked my current guardian angel to come back to my flat for a nightcap, she made a disastrous mistake. It was obvious that she knew exactly where I was staying, because she pressed the right lift button and headed for the right door — and there were three of them on my floor. When I remarked on this, she couldn't repress a guilty smile. She atoned for her blunder by spending the night with me, and, not being as angelic as she looked, she enjoyed herself as much as I did. Waiting to be infiltrated was proving a severe strain on my nerves, so nothing could have relaxed me more than the close proximity of her rosy-nippled breasts and shapely body, which she surrendered with abandon.

She had tiptoed out by the time I awoke, leaving behind her little khaki handkerchief as a memento. I never saw her again, but I mutely thanked her for the pleasure she had given me in the line of duty. Ever on the alert, I had concealed my true identity and my reasons for being in London, and the yarn I spun her about my activities as a commando sergeant must have amused the SOE security officers who had steered such a pretty girl in my direction.

★ ★ ★

In July, 1943, I received a second summons to present myself at Baker Street. On this occasion I was greeted by several officers and one civilian — an indication, I felt, that things were really moving at last. It wasn't until I returned to London in May, 1945, that General Colin Gubbins gave me a rundown on those who had been present. They included Major R. A. Bourne Patterson, officer i/c maps, Captain Gielgud, brother of John, the celebrated actor, John Senter, a lawyer and security specialist, Major Leslie Humphreys, and a young officer who seemed to be the general's right-hand man. The civilian I have never succeeded in identifying, but he spoke impeccable French.

I was congratulated on the good marks I had obtained at various schools, and reference was also made to the raid on Sark and its favourable outcome. Then I was asked the crucial question: Was I willing to go to Europe on a lengthy mission, one whose nature and duration presented considerable dangers?

If I accepted I would be parachuted into France at the next full moon, together with a wireless operator who spoke the language perfectly and would be personally assigned to me. The operation would be conducted blind, without a reception committee. I would be given a choice of several landing-places near Paris and the name and address of someone in the city to contact on arrival.

Having agreed, I was left alone with the two majors. After lunch, which was again served on the premises, we got down to business. The others not only outlined the preliminary phase of my mission but, to my surprise, invited me to express any reservations I might have and acquaint them with my own ideas. This genuine teamwork inspired me with complete confidence in my superiors. I was nevertheless aware that, once in the lion's den, I would often be left to fend for myself and could expect no help from them.

Humphreys explained that an alarming situation had developed within the Dutch Resistance, which had probably been penetrated by the Germans. In France the same suspicion attached to Resistance activities in the Bordeaux area, likewise to certain teams that handled the reception of agents and air drops. I was strictly forbidden to get in touch with any existing organizations. This meant that my mission was an extremely delicate one. I would be running big risks and playing with fire.

At the same time I would be able to pave the way for the main part of my mission, which was the establishment of a network entirely independent of all existing organizations, its task being to set up new escape and 'infiltration' routes extending from the north of Holland to the Spanish frontier and a route from Switzerland to Spain for the transportation of items of equipment destined for Britain. Humphreys gave me the names, addresses and passwords of persons who could assist me in Marseilles and at Delfzyl in the north of Holland. He then entrusted me to a FANY who drove me to a secret establishment outside London. I now knew too much and was classified as top security.

Fawley Court, my place of residence until I left England, was situated beside the Thames near Henley. Five other agents had already preceded me there. Though confined to the house and grounds, we were looked after like royalty, even to the extent of being regaled with fine vintage wines.

In one secluded wing of the house was a pleasant, spacious drawing-room whose french windows looked out on a well-tended lawn. Its furniture included some comfortable armchairs, a large table, and — an incongruous touch in such surroundings — a blackboard and a screen for the projection of slides. This was the briefing room where our final, detailed instructions were imparted. Other rooms in the same wing housed a wide assortment of clothing in every conceivable size.

On the day after my arrival I was introduced to two wireless operators and invited to choose between them. Without knowing that one of them was to accompany me, I had already made their acquaintance in the bar the night before and formed a preliminary opinion of them. After two brief conversations, I settled on Jacques Cornet. I was ignorant of his real name at Fawley Court, of course, and did not discover that it was Claude Planel until after the war.

Taller than I, who am only 5 feet 7 in my socks, Jacques was a swarthy, curly-headed young man who could have passed for a Corsican but was, in fact, a Mauritius-born British subject with an excellent knowledge of French. Jacques had been to university in England and gained a commission in the British Army before applying for a transfer to SOE. (He survived the war and now lives in retirement at Monte Carlo).

One of the tasks entrusted to Vera Atkins, Colonel Buckmaster's personal assistant, was to concoct, in consultation with the future agent, a 'legend' that would serve as his or her cover story. It was important to mingle fact with fiction, but without enabling enemy sleuths to unravel the thread that would lead them to the agent's true identity.

That was how I became 'Pierre Lalande', born at Arras (where the registers of births, marriages and deaths had been destroyed by German bombs in 1940) on 17 May, 1916. An only child, I had been orphaned at the age of six and brought up by an aunt who lived in Geneva. My parents had lost their lives in an accident during a trip to Senegal, where they were buried (an assertion which the Germans could not have checked in 1943). I had done my military service at Toulon, but only as an orderly-room clerk because, having broken my left arm as a boy, I was classified unfit for combat duty.

Called up and posted to the same unit in 1939, I had remained at Toulon until August, 1940 (the unit's records had disappeared when the Germans occupied the South of France). Thereafter I went to Paris and moved in with a young Swiss girl named Jacqueline, who worked at a big store there. Jacqueline had subsequently broken off our relationship and returned to her home near Geneva. Having obtained a job with Gaz de

Paris, the municipal gasworks, I was exempted from compulsory labour service in Germany. I lived in an attic bed-sitter at 96, rue de la Pompe, in the 16th arrondissement.

Such were the items of information I had to memorize until they were so ingrained that I myself believed in their authenticity.

The question of clothing was extremely important. To be arrested wearing a suit or shoes made in England was, of course, highly inadvisable. My own civilian clothes, which I had purchased in France and Belgium, were at the Stibbings' house, so I sent for them. All that had to be done was to remove a few tailors' labels and replace them with others emanating from French outfitters, of which Vera possessed a surprising number. My watch, wallet, fountain pen and cigarette case were all pronounced 'kosher'. All traces of tobacco from English or American cigarettes were removed from the case, and all my pockets, seams and linings were carefully cleaned.

Three days before the date scheduled

for our departure I paid another visit to London. This time my FANY driver took me to Orchard Court, Portman Square, where the whole day was devoted to running over the details of my mission.

Jacques and I would be parachuted into a field skirted by a country road on the edge of Fontainebleau Forest, some two kilometres from Fleury-en-Bière. We were to jump 'blind', which meant that no one would be waiting for us, and that we would have to make our way to Paris unaided. I was given the address of a 'friend' in Levallois-Perret, a Paris suburb, and the password that would serve to identify us.

I was to carry out the first part of my mission, which entailed visits to Switzerland and Holland, as rapidly as possible. Meantime, Jacques would find some good transmission sites in Paris or the suburbs.

The second part of the mission, which was just as urgent, was to set up some escape and infiltration routes for the use of SOE agents operating in Denmark, Holland, Belgium and France. Two additional contacts were given me: Per

Jensen at Delfzyl, and Thorkild Hansen, alias Berger, a Dane living on the outskirts of Marseilles. In parallel with the establishment of this network, I was to reconnoitre sites suitable for air drops of equipment and landing-grounds for the arrival and departure of agents by Lysander.

It was drawn to my attention that another SOE agent was already co-ordinating Lysander operations. This was Maurice Déricourt, alias Gilbert. Parachuted into central France six months earlier and now living in Paris with his wife, he concentrated his activities on the Loire area. Through the IS (Gilbert had infiltrated one of its agents in France) SOE had learned that, contrary to instructions, Gilbert had re-established contact with a pre-war friend, Oberstürmbannführer (SS Lieutenant-Colonel) Karl Boemelburg, a prominent member of the Gestapo in Paris. It was urgently necessary to set up a parallel network and then sever all connection with Gilbert. I myself was strictly forbidden to get in touch with him, and the same ban applied to all my old Marseilles friends from 1940 except the Reynauds.

The subsidiary task to be tackled on my first visit to Switzerland was the establishment of a network for the transportation of vital equipment from Yverdon, site of the Paillard precision instrument factories, to Barcelona in Spain.

One more item of information was communicated to me prior to my departure: I was startled but rather gratified to learn that I had been promoted captain. (Subsequently, because it was thought proper that I should outrank my wireless operator, I was upgraded to acting major, but I only held that rank while in the field.)

Finally, having been dismissed with a firm handshake and a 'Cheerio, good luck, see you on Liberation Day', I was driven back to Fawley Court with my mind in a whirl, wondering how I would ever manage to achieve what was expected of me.

★ ★ ★

Je tire ma révérence
et m'en vais au hasard,
sur les chemins de France,
de France et de Navarre . . .

This song, popularized by Jean Sablon, the so-called French Bing Crosby, haunted me as Jacques and I left Fawley Court for Tempsford. I was indeed about to 'make my bow and set off along the roads of France', but not, as the lyric implies, in a leisurely, aimless manner.

The first step was to double-check everything we carried on our persons. Stripped to the buff, we waited for our clothes to be minutely examined and returned to us. The same careful scrutiny was devoted to my French identity card in the name of Pierre Lalande, my ration cards, my Todt Organization permit certifying that I was employed by Gaz de Paris, a dog-eared letter from my former Swiss girlfriend, some snapshots of her soiled by their long sojourn next to my heart, one of her last letters bearing the German censor's stamp, and a Swiss Army knife she had given me when our love was new. Pierre Lalande was ready to depart.

After completing these formalities, we were allowed to visit the bar, where another three agents, one of them a young woman, were already leaning on the counter. The commandant of the base informed us that weather conditions over France looked good and that we would be taking off on schedule. He played host — we were allowed two drinks, no more — and shared our light supper, doing his best to relieve the tension by reeling off a string of jokes. The only member of the party too preoccupied to appreciate them was a Frenchman who had arrived in England the month before. His uneasiness was understandable: on the occasion of his only practice jump he had seen a man killed when his parachute failed to open.

Hugh Verity, the Lysander pilot whom I had already met while training at Tempsford, joined us for a few minutes. Aware that one of my tasks would be to reconnoitre potential landing strips, he gave me some useful tips on what to look out for. His parting words, as he slapped me on the back and bade us all farewell, were, 'See you in France one of these fine nights'.

Ten o'clock and time to go. We boarded a jeep for the few minutes' drive that would take us from Tempsford Manor to the corrugated iron huts on the edge of the airfield. The dark shape of our Halifax, parked on the apron near by and already being loaded, stood outlined against the night sky. I could just make out its identification letter, which was 'Q'.

There followed another last-minute check to ensure that we hadn't inadvertently pocketed a packet of English cigarettes or some other undesirable souvenir. We were given a stick or two of anonymous chewing-gum and a small flask of cognac.

With our jump-suits over our clothes and our parachutes strapped to our backs, we walked to the waiting aircraft. A resplendent moon was rising above the eastern skyline.

Before climbing aboard I stuck my chewing-gum to the ladder. One day, I thought, I would come back and retrieve it.

Blind Landing

Operation 'Bevy' was under way. The wheels of the Halifax left the tarmac and the aircraft slowly gained height. England dropped away beneath us. Seated on the floor of the freight compartment, all we could see through the open cockpit door was the glow of the instrument panel, but it was enough to banish our sense of total isolation.

The dispatcher, who had already flown eighteen similar sorties, understood the claustrophobic sensations that sometimes assailed his passengers. He switched on his torch and came and sat with us. A flask of brandy went the rounds.

The Halifax circled over Kent in a wide arc as it joined some other bombers preparing to unload their bombs on marshalling yards, factories or port installations. We were to take advantage of the 'cover' they afforded while crossing the Channel and the French coast.

Three-quarters of an hour went by. Then we heard the thud of exploding anti-aircraft shells and felt their blast jolt the fuselage. The roar of the engines helped to muffle the din outside. The pilot, Flying Officer Hart, reassured us over the intercom; by his standards this was a picnic.

Now that we had passed Dieppe and were well and truly in French air space we left the formation and flew much lower than before. After another twenty minutes the cockpit door was shut and the dispatcher removed the wooden lid covering the circular hole in the floor through which we would make our exit. We soared over the Loire and the town of Amboise, which showed up clearly in the moonlight. Visibility was so good that one could have seen a cat running across the street.

The dispatcher had dragged a big package over to the hole. We helped him to open it and jettison the content, which consisted of propaganda leaflets. They drifted down like birds, bringing messages of hope to those who were living under the German yoke. The co-pilot, who came aft to pay us a visit, explained that they were intended to mislead the enemy about the real reason for the presence of a lone aircraft.

A little further south we dropped some containers. When the Halifax was just short of the drop zone, which had been marked out with beacons by members of the Resistance, the navigator released them like bombs. Peering through the aperture occupied in a normal bomber by the forward lower gun turret, we could see the pinpoints of light slide past below us and the stick of containers floating down through the gloom on their parachutes.

Then we turned north-east, flew back over the Loire upstream from Montargis, and soon sighted a large expanse of wooded terrain, the Forêt d'Othe. We jettisoned another batch of leaflets over Sens. Fontainebleau Forest would come into view before long. Then it would be our turn to leave the plane.

My thoughts had strayed during the flight. They were partly of my unsuspecting family, so relatively near and yet so far, and partly of the task that lay ahead. Knowing the risks involved, would I be able to carry it out successfully? The 'blind' landing itself would be risky enough, but I had chosen to dispense with a reception committee — and my superiors had approved that decision — for two very definite reasons: first, to avoid contact with an existing network, and secondly to remain my own master. That way, any blunders I made would be down to me and no one else.

Jacques and I had been sitting beside the hole in the floor since Sens, looking down at the countryside. Now that the time had come, we felt surprisingly relaxed. The green light came on. I jumped first with Jacques so close behind that our parachutes were less than fifty metres apart. We could see the two chutes supporting our packages of equipment drifting down a considerable distance away. The silence was total, the landing perfect. We didn't even have to roll over.

The Halifax had receded into the darkness when we looked up. We were on our own now. I had come down in some stubble, Jacques on the edge of a field of uncut grain. Behind us was a small wood — just the place to bury our parachutes and jump-suits with the aid of the small, collapsible spades that formed part of our equipment.

That done, we carefully camouflaged the spot with dead leaves and branches and went in search of our packages. Fields of grain stretched away for as far as the eye could see. I climbed on my companion's shoulders for a better look. The parachutes should have been visible, but they weren't. We would have to make a snap decision. Wading through the uncut grain would leave telltale traces of our presence. A few hundred yards away we saw a farmhouse with a barn just this side of it. Though reluctant to put any more distance between us and the place where we presumed the packages had landed, we thought we might be able to see better from the roof of the barn. We hurried along the farm track that led to it, only to find that the roof was inaccessible. We mounted a harvester instead, but in vain: still nothing to be seen. To make matters worse, the moon disappeared behind a small cloud.

We had to take a risk. I knew that most of the local farmers, though not natural *résistants* because of their remoteness from the rigours of occupation, were loyal Frenchmen who would, in an emergency, find it in their hearts to help those who had set themselves the task of liberating their country. Besides, leaving our packages on their land would endanger them and lay them open to the suspicion of having assisted British agents.

I decided to scale the farmyard gate while Jacques waited outside, ready to make for Paris on his own if things went sour. I would have to be quick. It was nearly 2 a.m. by now, and first light was not too far off. Getting over the high, wrought-iron gate was child's play for an ex-commando, though a dog started barking in the yard. Hugging the walls, I stole toward the farmhouse with a pounding heart. Our entire mission might depend on what happened in the next few seconds. An upstairs window opened. 'Who's there?' called a voice. 'A friend in need of help,' I replied.

The front door opened an inch or two and the pyjama-clad farmer levelled a shotgun at my chest. His wife, hovering behind him with a shawl around her shoulders, was obviously expecting a child. They were a young couple little older than myself.

Very briefly, I explained that I had just landed by parachute and could not locate the packages that had followed me out of the plane. I didn't breathe a word about Jacques, just to be on the safe side.

'Let him in.' said the farmer's wife. 'We can't leave him standing there.'

My reluctant hosts were clearly alive to the danger of *agents provocateurs*, who were often unleashed on farming folk by neighbours envious of their relative prosperity, so it was only natural that they listened warily to my attempts to convince them of my bona fides. I could tell them very little, of course, being unable to disclose my destination and the purpose of my mission. The pistol I carried was a German Walther, and the cognac in my hip flask could have been purchased anywhere in France. Even my clothes had originated in France, as witness the labels sewn on in London.

Then I had a brainwave. My pockets contained some tablets for purifying water in case of need. I announced that they were cyanide pills for use if I was arrested by the Gestapo and suggested trying one out on the cat. That did the trick: the couple introduced themselves as Robert and Denise Pouteau and offered me a cup of coffee. Now that the atmosphere was more relaxed I told them that my wireless operator was waiting outside in the barn. We went to fetch Jacques, who joined us at the kitchen table. I could have broken down and wept, I felt so limp after all that nervous tension, but a good slug of brandy soon revived me.

I learned to my surprise that the Château de Fleury, the country house adjoining our hosts' farm, was occupied by a German army driving school. The Boches were just on the other side of the high wall that separated the two properties. My bosses certainly couldn't have been aware of this when they sanctioned my choice of landing-place!

Jacques and I had to get to Fontainebleau Forest before daybreak, so speed was essential. Robert Pouteau, ordained by fate to become the first member of my network (I gave him the code-name Édouard), had complete faith in the discretion of his farmhand, Lucien Carré.

172

Lucien was roused from his bed and joined us. I gave details of the aircraft's course, the packages' probable point of impact and the spot where our parachutes were buried. Robert undertook to recover the packages as soon as it was light and we agreed on a password to be used by the person who would come from Paris to collect them.

Robert advised us not to catch the bus from Barbizon, which was often subject to spot checks on the outskirts of Paris. Our best plan, he said, would be to disguise ourselves as campers, make our way through the forest on foot and hitch-hike when we reached the *route nationale*. He gave us some old cast-offs, a rucksack in which to stow our street clothes, which would have looked odd on campers, a knife and fork, some bread and cheese, and a bottle of water.

I knew the district well, fortunately, having camped in Fontainebleau Forest before the war, so hitting the *route nationale* at the Croix de Berny inter-section presented no problem. By 6 a.m. Jacques and I were taking our ease by the roadside, ready to thumb a lift from anyone going north. No luck, though. I got tired of waiting and decided to force the issue.

A vehicle appeared in the distance. I was already in the middle of the road when I saw that it was a Kubelwagen, a German military jeep, travelling with the hood down. Having committed myself, I stayed put. The Kubelwagen pulled up. The driver and his passenger were two Luftwaffe NCOs returning to their barracks at Orly.

I told them in German that we had been camping in the forest and had run out of money. Unable to afford the bus fare back to Paris, where we worked, we had spent the night in the open, hence our crumpled clothes and stubbly chins. The Germans laughed at our predicament and offered us a lift to Orly.

They were a jovial pair, and had obviously enjoyed a good night out. Prompted by their strong Bavarian accents, I described a visit to Munich in July, 1939, and paid tribute to the city's charms: the Hofbrauhaus, the coal-mining museum, the Oktoberwiese, the

Frauenkirche, the Feldherrenhalle. For good measure, I also told them how greatly I had been impressed by the cleanliness, good order and discipline that prevailed in the Third Reich. Jacques, who did not speak German, contributed to the atmosphere of mutual trust by smiling amiably. Cigarettes and chocolate were pressed on us.

We passed three check-points on the way to Paris without even slowing down. Our NCOs dropped us at a bus stop near their barracks and we parted with many protestations of Franco-German friendship. I couldn't help wondering what they would have said if they had known of our departure from England less than twelve hours before!

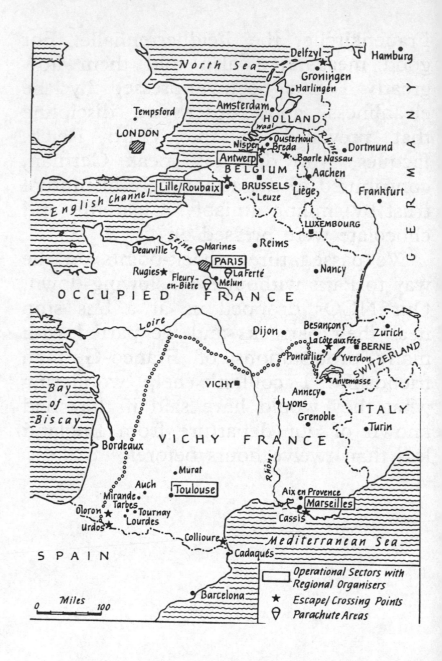

The Pierre-Jacques Network

11

The Pierre-Jacques Network

PARIS, alas, was the City of Light no longer. The coming of the Germans had changed all that. Although Jacques had carefully memorized its layout in advance, the French capital was new to him. Undeterred even by the caporal-and-garlic stench of the Métro, he found it a thing of beauty and a source of wonder. One immediate difference between Paris and London was that no signs of bomb damage could be seen.

From Orly we took a bus to Porte d'Italie, where we repaired to a café to sample our first ersatz coffee and change in the *toilettes*. We emerged unshaven but refreshed.

Édouard had provided us with some small change before we left the farm to save us from having to produce any of the large-denomination notes we had been given in London. It was time to head for Levallois-Perret, the Parisian suburb where our contact lived. We had been advised not to use any of the large Métro stations because they presented a greater risk of police checks, so we decided to walk.

The city's outward appearance had changed a great deal since my last visit three years earlier. The passers-by looked glum despite the summer sunlight that bathed the streets, and their clothes were worn and drab. The once ubiquitous taxicabs had been replaced by bicycle taxis and there were field-grey uniforms everywhere.

Our destination was a third-floor apartment in rue Marius-Aufan. It was just before midday when we rang the bell and asked for Monsieur Duquesne, claiming to be insurance agents with a policy for him to sign (our prearranged recognition signal). The woman who answered the door informed us that Duquesne was out, but that she was expecting him home for lunch if we cared to come back later. We thanked her and asked if we might leave our rucksack, which contained my Walther secreted inside a shoe.

We killed time in a Porte Champéret café over another so-called coffee with grape-pip sweetener, then tried again. Edmond Duquesne, known in our network as 'Doris', had returned. 'We've come about the fire insurance policy on your second home,' I began, but he had forgotten his prearranged response: 'The name of my cottage at Enghien is "Les Glycines".'

Although I felt a momentary pang of uncertainty, his physical appearance matched the description given us in London: a plump, balding, middle-aged bachelor of medium height. He had, in fact, grasped the reason for our presence as soon as he learned of our visit from his housekeeper, Geneviève Tourraine, the woman who had answered the door, and two extra places had already been laid for us. Lunch ended with a toast to final victory and the success of our mission.

It was two years since Doris had been persuaded by his friend Thorkild Hansen, my Danish contact in Marseilles, to assist Allied agents entering France for the purpose of organizing the Resistance. Although he had heard nothing since, he was happy to be able to keep his promise despite a certain understandable uneasiness about its potential hazards.

We recounted our adventures of the previous night and he immediately saw to it that our packages were collected. As a departmental head in Gaz de Paris he enjoyed access to certain facilities which the German authorities had granted that public utility company. Among these was a fleet of delivery vans authorized to operate up to 150 kilometres from Paris and issued by garrison headquarters with permits that exempted them from undergoing any unwelcome inspections. They returned to the capital laden with black market foodstuffs destined for the Gaz de Paris canteen and a small 'protected' restaurant patronized by German bigwigs with a taste for French *haute cuisine*. Jean Lesech, Doris's driver and right-hand man, a Breton who detested the Germans, was instructed to take one of these vans to Édouard's farm and pick up our packages.

Our first encounter with Doris was

notable for an alarming incident. I had taken my Walther from its hiding-place in the rucksack and removed the magazine, meaning to leave it with him for the time being. From force of habit I pulled the trigger, forgetting that this German-made weapon, unlike the Colt I used in the commandos, retained a round in the chamber. A shot rang out and a bullet embedded itself in the floor at my feet. We all froze, but nothing happened. Our fears slowly subsided. Vehicles propelled by charcoal gazogene burners tended to 'fart', as the French say, so the neighbours had probably mistaken the report for a backfire.

That left the problem of temporary accommodation. Madame Tourraine, whom we code-named Germaine, came up with the answer. She lived on the same floor, so she offered us one bed in her apartment and another in a maid's room on the top floor, under the slated roof.

We could now get down to serious business. Jacques was to remain in Paris and devote his time to finding suitable transmission sites. Meanwhile, having instructed Doris to organize the nucleus of a Paris network, I would travel to Switzerland to carry out the first part of my mission. I had to be back within ten days at most.

The Swiss Connection

At Veyrier, near Annecy, Doris had a cheese merchant friend whom he knew to be sympathetic to our cause. I did not have complete faith in the papers supplied me by London, so he procured me some more authentic ones made out in the name of André Lavigne, a representative of the Gaz de Paris canteen management. Armed with *Ausweise* bearing all the requisite German rubber stamps, I was officially going to Annecy, my staging-post for Switzerland, to negotiate the canteen's meat and cheese allocation. I decided to travel there by train and my papers survived their only inspection with ease. I felt reassured.

Auguste, the Veyrier cheese merchant, could not have been more helpful, though it is true that Doris had done him some substantial favours in the past. Something of a part-time smuggler, Auguste knew how to slip into Switzerland undetected. He accompanied me on the trip to the frontier, which we made partly by van and partly by bicycle. He also provided me with some Swiss money, which he never asked me to repay. Thanks to him, I got to Berne without difficulty by boarding a local train at Nyon, a few kilometres along the lake from Geneva.

Once in the Swiss capital, I called at the Dutch and British embassies in turn. My mission was an extremely important one because Britain's war industries were badly in need of Swiss precision instruments and, above all, of crystals for radio transmitters. The latter were exported by German factories based at Jena, officially for use in Switzerland itself.

One of the British embassy attachés had contacts with Autophon, a Zurich firm that manufactured telephone equipment using the said crystals, and with the Paillard factory at Yverdon. Paillard regularly supplied components to the Hispano Suiza works in Spain, which in turn manufactured engines for the German Army and Air Force. Consignments from Yverdon to Barcelona were sealed into German or Swiss lorries and driven across France to the Spanish border.

The problem was how to get packages destined for England into these consignments and disguise them. On arrival at the Hispano works they would be spirited away by the SOE agents employed there and forwarded to Gibraltar, or sometimes to Lisbon.

I was given the name of the Paillard director to contact at Yverdon and left to get on with it. A man in his mid-sixties, he was decidedly pro-British and had been on very friendly terms with the former British consul in Basle, Sir Frank Nelson. I spent two pleasant evenings as his guest but did not show my face at the factory itself, German spies being thick on the ground in Switzerland.

We duly worked out the system in detail. Crystals from Germany and gadgets manufactured by Autophon would be delivered via Zurich to the Paillard factory at Yverdon. There, concealed among crates of other equipment, they would be secreted in consignments bound for Hispano at Barcelona.

I remain convinced, from his intimate knowledge of British methods, that my host had connections with the Intelligence Service. He also knew what routes to use when sneaking into France, and drove me to a spot near the Côte aux Fées. From there, making my way through a densely wooded area, I was able to slip across the frontier without running into the Swiss or German patrols that guarded it. Once in France I was to go to a café just short of La Cluse, where I would be helped on my way to Paris.

I found the place without any awkward encounters. The *patron* advised me not to catch a train at Pontarlier. Instead, he drove me in a timber lorry to Lons-le-Saunier, where there was less danger of spot checks. I was back in Paris on the evening of the eighth day after my departure.

Teething Troubles

Jean Lesech, alias Lucien, had picked up our packages of equipment from Fleury-en-Bière during my absence, so Jacques was now in possession of his transmitters and had already sent three messages to London. 'Raymond', an Argenteuil butcher whose real name was René Picotin, had been appointed his bodyguard, and Jacques had chosen to base himself at Raymond's home. The two men became close friends in the course of time. They were an incongruous pair. Jacques was a well-organized young man, calm and systematic in his work; Raymond was true Parisian 'Cockney', full of courage, humour and native wit, but he tended to do hare-brained things and had to be kept on a tight rein.

'Hector', another friend of Doris, was abbé of the Église de la Trinité. Henri Jeglot by name, he was a very worldly churchman with access to high society and theatrical circles. My first rendezvous with him took place in a confessional. Hesitant and unconvinced at first, Hector didn't demonstrate his abilities to the full until I got the BBC to broadcast a personal message for him: 'The abbé has grey slippers'. Thereafter he proved a valuable and courageous associate.

My first problem was to find some safe-houses in Paris. Having been offered ten or more such addresses in less than a week, I selected the nine that afforded the best means of escape in an emergency. One of them was a short-time hotel in rue de Provence 'sanctioned' by the German authorities, who patronized it regularly. Another was a house near the Parc Monceau used for lovers' assignations. The Church's contacts are indeed many and various!

In addition to an apartment in boulevard Péreire, I retained three of the above addresses for my personal use. Situated in widely separated parts of Paris, they provided me with bolt-holes if I was overtaken by a curfew. Being entirely remote from my network's other activities, they also enabled me to confer with agents in peace when they came to submit their reports. The other addresses served as dead letter-boxes or accommodation for birds of passage.

Lucien's brother-in-law, Maxime Masure, was employed at the town hall in La Courneuve, a northern suburb of Paris. Code-named Marcel, he was a secure source of aids to the fabrication of authentic-looking false papers and ration cards. He even, on occasion, lent us some police uniforms.

Lucien Lobin, alias Léon, was a printer in Faubourg Possonnière. *Ausweise* and rubber stamps of all kinds were produced in his backyard print-shop, which communicated with two other buildings whose exits came out in another street. One of his employees, an elderly veteran of the 1914 – 18 war, was a true artist, and the only real problem was how to obtain paper of a quality similar to that of genuine documents.

Three weeks had gone by since my arrival, twenty-one crowded days and nights during which, among other things, I had scouted an air-drop site and a landing-ground suitable for Lysanders. With September approaching and the nucleus of a Paris network firmly established, my next concern was to set up a route to Spain. The SOE authorities were a demanding and impatient bunch and everything had to be done in double-quick time. My new focus of effort entailed a series of trips to the south.

The Pyrenean Pipeline I

I had been strictly forbidden to make use of my former contacts in Marseilles, which didn't help. All that Baker Street had given me was the address of a smuggler based at Urdos in the department of Basses-Pyrénées, together with a warning that professional *passeurs* of his type had often been known to play a double game. Apart from that rather depressing information, I would be groping in the dark.

Once again it was Abbé Jeglot, alias Hector, who came to my assistance. Armed by him with a letter addressed to the father superior of a neighbouring monastery, I travelled to Lourdes as an auxiliary nurse accompanying some cripples and invalids who were going there on a pilgrimage. Not for the first time, it astonished me to discover the extent to which right-thinking individuals were willing to commit themselves on behalf of a just cause.

The father superior considered it his sacred duty to assist and shelter me. When I disclosed that Urdos was my chosen transit point on the route to Spain, he pointed out that it was situated in another archdiocese, that of Toulouse. After making a telephone call, he told me to go there and ask for the archbishop himself, Monseigneur Saliège, who would be expecting me.

I took a bus from Lourdes to Toulouse, travelling via Tarbes, and was greeted at the archdiocesan offices by Canon Paul Dessort, the vicar-general, who fixed me an appointment with the archbishop after early Mass the next day. When I told him I had nowhere to stay he found me a bed at the home of a fellow cleric.

My interview with Monseigneur Saliège was brief but to the point. He telephoned to inquire the name of the abbé of Urdos and strongly recommended me to look up the curé of Saint-Christau, Abbé Salefranque, for whom he gave me a message. I was to go first to Urdos and then, in the event of failure, to Saint-Christau.

Urdos was a sizeable village situated beside the Gave d'Aspe between Oloron-Sainte-Marie and the Spanish frontier. To avoid retracing my steps to Tarbes by train, I took three uncomfortable, ramshackle buses in succession. There were few Germans to be seen except in Toulouse itself, where my papers were checked as I left.

I got to Urdos at nightfall on 1 September, 1943, and knocked on the door of the presbytery. The abbé's housekeeper opened it a few inches. '*Monsieur le curé n'est pas là*,' she told me curtly, but she let me in when I told her I came from Monseigneur Saliège, Archbishop of Toulouse. 'One has to be careful with all these Catalan refugees about,' she grumbled in explanation.

The abbé had gone off to a distant farm to administer extreme unction to a dying man, but supper was already prepared. I must have looked famished, because the housekeeper relented and sat me down at table.

It was late when Abbé Usaurgu finally appeared, spattered with mud because it had been raining and his bicycle had lost its mudguards. An ascetic-looking man in his late thirties, Usaurgu was as Basque as his name. He stared at my unfamiliar face in surprise, but greeted me like a long-lost friend when he heard who had sent me.

We talked far into the night. Once assured of the curé's patriotism — Usaurgu was no Vichyite and had already helped several Jewish refugees to cross the frontier — I disclosed the purpose of my visit. When I also confided that I had been in London only six weeks before, his face lit up. He hurried downstairs to the cellar, and two bottles of good Bordeaux made their appearance on the table.

Usaurgu threw up his arms at the name of the smuggler London had recommended. It seemed that many of those who had used the man as a guide had never reached their destination, and the curé was convinced that they had been robbed and murdered on the way. Such, in any case, was the local rumour.

I could not stay long, unfortunately, but by noon the next day Usaurgu was able to tell me that I could go on my way with an easy mind. The passwords to be used had been agreed, as had the place and person in Spain to which 'passengers' would be conducted. My lucky star had once more steered me in the right direction.

I decided to return via Marseilles in order to call on Thorkild Hansen, alias Henri Berger, and inform him of the outcome of my expedition. By 5 September I was back in Paris.

The Astrakhan Coat

In addition to lodging at rue Marius-Aufan with Edmond Duquesne, alias Doris, during my first month in Paris, I had already found three families willing to let me spend the night on their premises. My presence was a permanent source of danger to them, however, and I wanted to minimize that danger by looking for an apartment where I could live alone. My cover as an insurance inspector accorded me a status that would enable me to live in some comfort.

I asked Abbé Jeglot, that worldly-wise and well-connected priest, to find me an apartment to rent. Through him I learned that the French entertainer Maurice Chevalier, referred to in the network as 'Valentine', was on friendly terms with an actress who cohabited with a German, a high-ranking Gestapo officer who had been posted to the German embassy in Madrid and wanted her to accompany him there. She was anxious to sublet her apartment at once, with the result that, late one afternoon, I found myself discussing the terms of the lease at 199 Boulevard Péreire.

The German haggled on his girlfriend's behalf with a tenacity that would have done credit to an Armenian carpetseller. I had to purchase all the fixtures and fittings, not only in pesetas but at black market prices. Although it was hard to get hold of the Spanish currency in time, everything was settled within two days. The German had already departed for Spain when I signed the sublease in the presence of the actress and her landlord.

Before I left, my hostess invited me to have 'a cup of tea' with her. She went off to make it and returned in a flimsy negligé that left no doubt of her intentions. Although she wasn't my type, being some years older and rather on the fleshy side, I swallowed my reservations with good grace.

At the end of the afternoon, when we'd exhausted our amatory repertoire, I discovered what underlay her sudden passion for me. 'I need some money for myself. The fixtures and fittings belong to my boyfriend, so I'll have to give him the money you've paid me. I've got an astrakhan coat which I won't be needing in Spain. It's worth a hundred and twenty-five thousand francs — you simply must buy it.'

And that was how I became the reluctant owner of an astrakhan coat.

Maryse

Anyone leading the double life of an agent must wear a cloak of normality and behave in keeping with his age and official occupation. I was well-provided in the latter respect, with opportunities for travel and valid reasons for being away from home. However, a normal young bachelor should also have a social life. A girlfriend was essential not only to my façade but also to my mental well-being, so I had to find myself one.

Alongside rue de Courcelles there was a

small expanse of grass with park benches, the Square Sainte-Odile, which I often passed on my way to see the verger of the nearby church, who acted as one of my 'letter-boxes'. That was where I first met Maryse.

A children's nurse of Polish origin, Maryse regularly went walking there with the two little boys in her charge. She had a pretty face and was far from shy, as I deduced when I heard her chatting in their own tongue with some German soldiers. I gave her a smile, played football with the boys, introduced myself and invited her to come to the cinema with me.

Maryse, who was employed by a couple who lived in rue de Courcelles, occupied an attic room on their premises. I learned from the verger that they were notorious collaborators. This was all to the good, because it enabled me to combine business with pleasure and enhance my own collaborator's 'cover' at 199 Boulevard Péreire. Two framed photographs appeared on my walls, one of Marshal Pétain and the other of Laval welcoming a delegation from the fascist

Légion Française contre le Bolchevisme.

Maryse's employers, who seemed to take an almost parental interest in their nanny and wanted to know who was 'walking out' with her, invited me to supper one night. I had to lie my head off, but it all helped to reinforce my façade.

In the belief that I sometimes traded on the black market, Maryse once set a trap for me, probably at her employers' instigation, because her story sounded rather unconvincing: she asked if I could get hold of some gold for her dentist.

Maryse was the only person who had access to my flat apart from Madame Tourraine, who came to clean it once a week.

Could she have been responsible for the disappearance of my hard-earned astrakhan coat? I suspect so, though I never found out for certain.

The Scarlet Pimpernel of the Airwaves

The Scarlet Pimpernel, that classic adventure story, describes how an English aristocrat kept the French police on the hop at the time of the Revolution. 'They seek him here, they seek him there, those Frenchies seek him everywhere . . . '

History repeated itself in the days of the Resistance, as the following episode demonstrates.

In 1943 the Germans stepped up their efforts to locate clandestine radio transmitters. Their usual practice was to pinpoint the source of a signal by cross-bearings, which they very quickly managed to do with the aid of three detector vans.

The initial method of detection had been to cut off the electricity supply in the predetermined sector, thereby halting transmission and informing the Germans of the general area in which the radio was located. This trick was soon discovered and countered, however. A telltale was inserted in the circuit, and the transmitter switched over to batteries.

The problem of detector vans was harder to cope with because they were disguised as vehicles belonging to local firms, and even the lookouts posted in neighbouring streets sometimes failed to spot them. If they did raise the alarm and transmission ceased abruptly, it not only delayed the passing of messages but told the Germans that the transmitter was close at hand.

That was how, at my suggestion, the wireless expert Clément Billard, alias Robert, came to devise the 'Scarlet Pimpernel' system, which entailed using three transmitters several kilometres apart. The prime essential was to have good telephonic communication between the three and two lookouts per ghost transmitter, so that we could promptly switch from one radio to another if danger threatened.

The ghost transmissions were figments of my imagination drafted in a code which the enemy could easily decipher. They sent the Germans scurrying all over the place in search of nonexistent air drops or rendezvous.

Billard's technique certainly enraged the German radio-detection service, to the delight of the lookouts who saw its dread vehicles drive off, leaving the main transmitter to continue sending in peace. It was employed with success for many months.

Left, right, left . . .

Clothing shortages had certain repercussions in occupied France. To minimize wear and tear on shoes, most people — including me — had taken to reinforcing them with metal heel and toe plates, like tap-dancers.

Since I tended to march along on my heels in a typically military fashion, my footsteps were readily identifiable. Every man has his own way of walking and the sound becomes even more noticeable at night.

I often returned to my Boulevard Péreire apartment at a late hour, sometimes even after curfew, and my usual route took me past a police post. One night a gendarme hailed me through the door, which was open. I was carrying no incriminating papers, fortunately, having just walked Maryse home, but I felt a twinge of alarm as I paused and turned to him. 'Monsieur,' he said, 'we recognize your footsteps every time you walk past. It could land you in trouble, because we often receive visits from our "protectors". You should be more careful.' By 'protectors', of course, he meant the German police or their hated French confederates. I continued on my way with a sigh of relief.

Did the worthy gendarme sense that I was a *résistant*? I never found out, but it comforted me to know that at least one Paris policeman was not in sympathy with the occupying power.

After that I removed my heel plates and padded along like a cat.

More Peregrinations

Doris had not been idle. He introduced me to Eugène Vannier, a regional representative of the La Flandre insurance company based at Lille, whose work enabled him to move around a great deal in the departments of Nord and Pas-de-Calais, and even as far afield as Ardennes. Vannier also paid a weekly visit to the company's head office in Paris. All these perfectly legitimate business trips made him a very useful associate and, from my point of view, an ideal regional organizer. I spent three days training him — not long, but he was so intelligent, conscientious and discreet that I threw him in at the deep end without any qualms. Code-named Valentin, he set up safe-houses and dead letter-boxes and organized the guides and contacts who formed that section of our network which helped to smuggle agents across the Belgian frontier in either direction. Among those who made use of this pipeline were French, Belgian, Dutch, Danish and British agents.

My next task was to extend the network into the Low Countries. The insurance company operated in Belgium as well, and it was as a head office representative from Paris that I made my first trip there, armed with one of the celebrated pink *Ausweise* that entitled their holders to cross the frontier an unlimited number of times. Lobin had forged me some new papers in the name of a director of La Flandre, only the date of birth and photograph being my own.

At Lille I recruited Paul Péfau, code-named Philippe I, together with my old friend from Marseilles, Paul Eckmann, alias Émile, and his brother Pierre, who adopted the code-name Edmond.

Philippe I became second-in-command to Valentin, my regional organizer, while Émile functioned as a recruiting officer and Edmond as a courier between Lille and Roubaix, where the brothers lived. I personally tested our first operational crossing-point at Wattrelos by making a return trip to Belgium. Wattrelos and Herseaux, where Dr Delmas acted as *passeur*, were to become our principal crossing-points.

Early the next day I went to Tournai, in the south of Belgium, and caught a train for Brussels. I got out at Hal, a small town fifteen kilometres from there, so as to avoid any awkward checks at the Gare du Midi. My knowledge of the German check-points at that station was only sketchy, so it was better to be doubly careful the first time.

I felt an involuntary pang of sadness on re-entering the city that was home to the parents with whom I could not, under present circumstances, be reunited. Only they and their closest friends knew that I was supposed to be in England. My own friends, whose last news of me dated from 1940, believed that I was still somewhere in France. Much as it distressed me to remain incognito, I had no wish to expose my parents to danger or burden them with the knowledge that I was risking life and liberty in occupied territory.

Guy Andrin, a schoolfriend of mine, lived at Forest, near the Place de l'Altitude Cent. I had known him for so long and was so certain of his discretion that I paid him a visit. Although I never invited him to join my network, a task for which he was psychologically unfitted, he did me a great service by putting me in touch with people who could provide safe-houses in Brussels and Leuze. He also had an army friend who became a courageous associate of mine. This was Commandant Auguste Soffie, already a member of the Belgian military resistance organization, who regularly supplied me with the identity cards, *Ausweise* and other documents required by my network. It was through him that I subsequently established an outstation in the village of Battice, on the road from Liège to Aachen. I earmarked it for future operations that might even have extended into German territory. It never became fully operational and I paid only one visit to the premises, a small garage, but its owner, code-named Theo, became a regular source of information about German troop movements. London may later have employed him direct, because he did not survive the war. The Germans shot him prior to the liberation of Belgium.

No Peace for the Wicked

Having set up this embryonic branch of the network, I returned to Paris for a brief spell of relaxation. The last five weeks had been exceptionally tiring and I had to satisfy myself that all was running smoothly in France. I also had a great deal of information to transmit to London. In fact, my hopes of relaxation were illusory. Bombarded with problems by every member of the network I encountered, I was expected to solve them on the spot.

For reasons of security, I had taken no notes of what I had been doing in the previous three weeks, so it was a considerable test of memory to recall it all for my bosses, who were fretting like lions at feeding time. Although Jacques had radioed them that I was away on a trip, that terse message had only served to alarm them, because I was normally expected to make at least one sign of life every week. They were reassured by the mountain of data I sent them, however, and their reprimands gave way to congratulations.

It was a tedious job encoding messages many pages long, and Jacques remained chained to his Morse key for three whole days, dashing from one transmission site to another to avoid being pinpointed by German D/F vans. London was certainly quick to digest all these messages, because the first 'exfiltration' candidate, a Dutchman code-named Joris, turned up in Brussels on 2 October.

Our sphere of operations now extended for more than fifteen hundred kilometres, as the crow flies, and our main transmitter was situated in the Paris area. This meant that, although we used couriers, most of whom were not formal members of the organization and received payment for their services, speed of communication was the principal problem to be solved if our network was to function as it should.

Not for the first time, it was Abbé Jeglot who found the answer. He had recruited Suzanne Budelot, alias Simone, who not only provided a safe-house for agents in transit but proved even more useful to me in other respects. Secretary to the board of the SNCF (Société *Nationale des Chemins de Fer*) in rue Saint-Lazare, she introduced me to various heads of department at the Gares du Nord, de Lyon, de l'Est, Montparnasse, and Saint-Lazare, of whom Monsieur Lèble, code-named Lola, was particularly active. It was they who provided me with the couriers I so badly needed from among the main-line train crews, many of whom, I surmise, were also members of the 'Fer' (railwaymen's) Resistance network. Of twenty-three people engaged in this activity, only one vanished without trace.

But Simone rendered me another important service: she used to procure train tickets for me, thereby exempting me from having to draw attention to myself while standing in the long queues that often formed in those wartime days. This stood me in good stead on several occasions, notably when London requested me to set up a second route into Spain.

The Pyrenean Pipeline II

I took a train to the south once more. Saint-Christau, the place that had been recommended to me by Monseigneur Saliège, was a small village some forty kilometres from Pau. I had already travelled that way when visiting Urdos, twenty-five kilometres to the south, but it was no easy matter to get there in October, 1943. More isolated and not immediately adjacent to the frontier, Saint-Christau seemed to have all the makings of a good assembly-point for persons on their way to Spain. Issaux Forest offered good cover, and a number of tracks led south from the village of Arrette-Pierre-Saint-Martin, whence it was an easy matter to make for Huesca in Spain.

The last bus had left when I got to Oloron, in the heart of the anti-German Pays Basque, so I decided to walk the last ten kilometres. It would be good exercise, and the picturesque road led through Pyrenean scenery bright with autumn colours.

Saint-Christau turned out to be a diminutive hamlet, nothing more. I'd been told that it boasted some hot springs, but there was no sign of any spa, just a church so small that it resembled a chapel. The door was open and candles were burning in front of a statue of Saint-Personne (St Nobody!). I was sweating hard after my long walk, so I fled the chilly interior and sought the warmth of the sun.

An old Basque, seated on a bench outside the church, eyed me closely. 'Looking for the *curé*? He'll be back in time for vespers.' That meant a four-hour wait, and I hadn't eaten a thing since lunch the day before. To kill time I went for a stroll. Stretching out on a grassy bank at the edge of a small wood, I propped my head on my suitcase and dozed off.

I was roused by a tap on the leg with a walking-stick. An old priest in a worn cassock was standing over me. His keen eyes surveyed me from head to foot. I must have made a favourable impression, because he smiled and said, 'You wanted to see me? Very well, come along.'

I followed him to the door of the sacristy, where he inquired the purpose of my visit. I said he had been recommended to me by Canon Dessort of Toulouse. 'Ah, yes,' the old man replied, 'he mentioned you to me, and you fit the description he gave. You must be hungry. Come with me.'

Over a welcome meal Abbé Salefranque listened with interest to what I had to say. Yes, he told me, several of his flock were capable of doing the job I had in mind, but he himself would remain my sole contact. His negotiations with those who expressed their willingness to smuggle people across the frontier were conducted in Basque, a language wholly unintelligible to me. They were to be paid by him when they returned from such trips, but only on production of some object, different each time; given

210

them by the SOE agent who had taken charge of the 'passengers' on their arrival in Spain. The abbé did not entirely trust professional *passeurs*. They were in it for the money, but he knew they would never denounce him personally. Like mafiosi, the petty crooks of the Pays Basque had their own code of honour.

* * *

The Mediterranean has its attractions, even in November. My next trip was to Collioure, a pretty little fishing village with an ancient castle and a 13th-century monastery. Pierre Goalabré, an assistant of my regional organizer at Marseilles, had gone there ahead of me to set up a maritime escape route to Spain. Though officially prohibited, fishing at night *a lámpara* was such a tradition that the local authorities continued to tolerate it. Once at sea, clandestine passengers would be transferred to a Spanish fishing-boat and landed at a small bay near Cadaqués, whence they would make their way to Barcelona.

Before engaging in this risky trade, the

211

two fishermen in question had insisted on negotiating the 'fare' with someone in authority. The security system adopted was the same as the one I had established at Urdos and Saint-Christau, but I do not know, to this day, whether effective use was ever made of this route because it was entirely controlled by Henri Berger, my regional organiser at Marseilles.

★ ★ ★

An alarming incident occurred on my return journey to Paris. When we pulled into Lyons-Perrache I was perturbed to see armed German soldiers station themselves on the platform outside every carriage door. Simultaneously, a group of men boarded the train — men whose civilian clothes stamped them quite unmistakably as members of the Gestapo. It was clear that they were looking for someone, possibly me.

I couldn't afford to let them examine my papers. Quickly borrowing a white jacket from a dining-car steward, who, though startled, relinquished it without a word, I grabbed a crate of empty bottles

212

In uniform once more – the author, 1945.

Thurso, 1942 – Commando amphibious training. *(Author)*

My Commando Service Certificate.

**COMMANDO
SERVICE CERTIFICATE**

Italy	Crete	Burma	Greece
Norway	France	Sicily	Albania
Holland	Belgium	Germany	Madagascar
North Africa	Yugoslavia	Western Desert	Channel Islands

This Certificate is an Appreciation,
of Loyal Service given to Commandos by

Lieutenant Lembch Schreve.

March 1942

R. Laycock.

Chief of Combined Operations

No. 12 Commando.
No. 10 I.A. Commando. 2 Dutch Troop
May 1943

Linxel.
Commanding officer.

Prince Bernhard of the Netherlands visits our 2 Troop
Club at Portmadoc. Our former Troop Commander,
Captain Mulder, is with the Prince, author second from
right. *(Dutch Commando Museum)*

Major-General Colin
Gubbins, Head of SOE
1942-46. *(SOE Archives)*

Vera Atkins, Intelligence
Officer, French Section,
SOE. *(SOE Archives)*

The only photograph of the hub of the Pierre-Jacques Network. *Left to right:* Edmond Duquesne (Doris), Claude Panel ('Jacques') and the author ('Pierre'). *(Author)*

A drawing by the author of the entrance to Buchenwald. *(Archives Nationales)*

BUCHENWALD

" Recht oder unrecht,... mein Vaterland "

DORA – part of the camp after the evacuation and the arrival of the American troops.
(National Archives, Washington)

DORA – one of the entrances to the N1 tunnels. In the foreground are V2 liquid oxygen vessels.
(National Archives, Washington)

SS *Sturmbannführer*
(Major) Otto Förschner,
the first Commandant of
DORA. *(War Crimes Commission,*
KX Gedenkstätte Dachau)

Josef Killian, the official
hangman in DORA. Not
an SS-man but a 'green'
German inmate.
(War Crimes Commission)

SS *Obersturmführer*
(Lieutenant) Moeser –
the man who showed
no remorse. Camp
Commandant of
DORA and leader of
the 'death convoy' to
Ravensbrück.
(War Crimes Commission)

Part of the group that escaped from the column leaving Ravensbrück and reached the Elbe. Here, washed, fed and kitted out by the Dutch in Enschede, we are standing in front of the truck given to us by the Americans. *(Author)*

With my father, September 1945. *(Author)*

and got down on the platform. The sentry, who assumed that I was going to replenish the dining-car's stock of wine, waved me past. I disappeared into the washroom of the station restaurant where I dumped the crate and jacket. My own coat and my suitcase, which contained nothing compromising, remained on board the train and doubtless found a new home.

'Rose', a restaurateur and local member of the network, put me up for the night. The next morning I calmly caught the same train and continued on my way to Paris. It had been a close shave.

Back to the Low Countries

Late that autumn I set out to strengthen the sector of my network covering Belgium and Holland. With that in mind, I contacted the Demeuse family at Antwerp, whom I had known since childhood because my father had helped them to find a temporary refuge in neutral Holland during the 1914 – 18 war.

There was a certain risk in recruiting people who knew my real identity, but I took it without hesitation. For one thing I had no alternative; for another the Demeuses were ignorant of my sojourn in England. They welcomed me warmly, as if I had at last returned from the South of France, where my father had told them I was living. When I broached the subject of the German occupation, I found that, although not a member of the Resistance because he mistrusted those who had invited him to join it, Monsieur Demeuse was wholly in sympathy with those who risked their lives on its behalf.

After dinner, when his wife and daughter had tactfully withdrawn, I disclosed the true purpose of my visit and asked him, straight out, if he would be willing to become my regional organizer for Belgium and extend the network into Holland, where he had some potentially useful contacts. He promptly agreed, and I code-named him 'Ernst'. When the women rejoined us he said it was too late for me to return to Brussels and invited me to stay the night.

I remained with the Demeuses for four days, during which time I familiarized my new recruit with his duties and made a brief excursion across the Dutch border. A trustworthy friend of Ernst's accompanied me on this cycle ride. My borrowed machine was typically Dutch, a lofty contraption fitted with a saddle as hard as iron, and the return trip of some 60 kilometres took us through woods and along dirt roads to the Dutch frontier village of Nispen. Ernst's friend knew all the minor roads and check-points on the outskirts of Essen, the Belgian frontier village a few kilometres from our destination, and we reached there without incident.

One of Ernst's relations, Vandeven by name, owned a general store much patronized by the frontier guards. We already knew that the Vandevens were loyal to the Dutch Crown, and when I told them that I had actually met Princess Juliana and her daughters (the elder of whom is now Queen of the Netherlands) they promptly agreed to help us. Monsieur Vendeven, whom I code-named Victor, had relatives at Roosendaal and Nieuw Gastel. He set up a meeting for the same afternoon in the latter village, which was not far away.

It proved successful. In less than five hours we had forged an important link in our chain: a *passeur* and two safe-houses capable of absorbing future traffic, which promised to be heavy. As my organizer at Antwerp, Ernst would supervise it and issue any instructions required to keep it functioning smoothly.

I pedalled back to Antwerp and went to bed that night with a sense of achievement which not even the bruises inflicted on my backside by the adamantine bicycle saddle could blight, ready to continue operations on the morrow and extend the network deeper into Holland.

My previous day's training stood me in good stead because I had an even longer distance to cover, this time accompanied by Irma, Ernst's daughter, whom I had also recruited. Our destination was Breda, where a schoolteacher friend of Ernst's, now dead, had lived before the war. Ernst had kept in touch with Madam Vink, his late friend's sister, and it was to her pretty little house outside Oosterhout that we now pedalled in the teeth of a fierce, rain-laden gale that soaked us to the skin.

The door was opened by Monsieur Vink. He was glad to see the daughter of one of his Belgian friends and Irma introduced me to him as a member of the family. Close to retirement age, Vink was a quiet, austere-looking man who weighed his words carefully. He was also very religious, and, it being Sunday, I was obliged to attend evensong at the local church. Having broached the subject of the Dutch Resistance during the afternoon, I already knew that his wife distributed clandestine newspapers. Unlike him, she was a jolly, rather outgoing person.

I decided to mention the network at supper on our return from church. Like many of my compatriots, Vink was wary and suspicious by nature. To reassure him, I offered to get the BBC to broadcast a personal message when I returned to Paris. It was his wife who convinced him and tipped the scales. I asked her, for safety's sake, to stop distributing clandestine literature.

I appointed Andreas, as I code-named

Vink, co-ordinator of our operations in Holland, a task for which he possessed all the requisite qualifications, and told him that Ernst would pass on all the directives and principles of organization in which I had schooled him. Although I saw Andreas only once more, he proved that my faith in him had not been misplaced.

The Network Completed

Back in Paris I found a mass of signals awaiting me in my personal code. Although London had known of my absence, there was no way they could have been forwarded to me. The only possible solution to this problem was to entrust my regional organizers with greater responsibility so that London could, in an emergency, communicate with them direct if I was away for more than a certain number of days. All this extra but unavoidable work could have been spared had I possessed an assistant capable of replacing me, but SOE was reluctant to send me one. 'Do your best,' was the only response to my request.

The upshot was that my regional heads were made fully accountable for their own sphere of operations and enjoyed a certain measure of independence. The following organization came into being, each sector having its own code and its own identification:

- *The Paris region*, which was also in charge of landing-grounds for Lysanders and air drops;
- *The south-east sector* centred on Marseilles, which covered Cassis, Lyons, the Collioure sea-route, and the 'merchandise' route from Switzerland to Spain;
- *The south-west sector* based at Toulouse, which supervised the Pyrenean crossing-points, Mirande, and contacts with the maquis of Murat;
- *The northern sector*, covering the Lille area, Roubaix, and the crossing-points on the Belgian frontier;
- *The Belgium-Holland sector* centred on Antwerp and in charge of operations in both these countries.

Thanks to the courage and determination of all those brave men and women who had answered my calls for assistance, the Pierre-Jacques network was now up and running.

12

An Agent's Life

NOVEMBER, 1943, came, and with it a request from London: I was to go to the British embassy in Berne to interrogate two Dutch agents who claimed to have escaped from the Gestapo in Holland and reached Switzerland by way of Paris. My task would be to verify their statements and the authenticity of their escape network.

I set off for Switzerland, travelling via Haute-Savoie as before. Everything went without a hitch. The story told by the agents, whose names were Dourlien and Ubbink, seemed plausible, and I reported as much to London via the Berne embassy. All that remained was to double-check it in Paris and Holland, just to eliminate every last doubt, because it was possible that they had become double agents released by the SD in the hope of penetrating the British secret services in England itself. I entrusted this job to Paul Eckmann, who acquitted himself extremely well. In January I was able to radio London that I considered both agents thoroughly trustworthy.

★ ★ ★

In November I received a message warning me to expect an air drop. I could not be present because of prior commitments, but I had complete confidence in the team that was to form the reception committee. The BBC duly broadcast a message informing us that the operation was under way: 'The abbé has two grey slippers.' The word 'two' signified that an agent would be dropped as well as some containers.

Rest in Peace, Friend

The night sky was clear, but a strong wind had sprung up at ground level and landing would be tricky. If I had been present myself I might well have cancelled the air drop, despite the annoyance this would have caused in London. By the time the head of the reception committee to have his doubts it was too late.

The parachutist, who left the aircraft first, was carried some distance from the landing-ground by a sudden gust of wind. The two men sent to retrieve him found that he had come down heavily in a ditch and been dragged along it for nearly a hundred metres. Dead by the time they reached him, he had sustained multiple injuries and broken his neck. They bore him off to a nearby barn while the rest of the party recovered the containers.

The owners of the barn were reluctant to keep or bury the body, so it was decided to take it to Paris for disposal. The reception committee had been provided with a Gaz de Paris van driven by Jean Lesech, whom we met earlier, and regularly passed the German check-point at the Porte de Clichy without being inspected. The guard commander, who was used to seeing the vehicle return to the French capital laden with food from the country, usually received a small edible gift whenever it came his way.

The contents of the containers were

hidden beneath a layer of meat and vegetables. As for the dead man, he was muffled up in an overcoat and wedged into the passenger seat with a broad-brimmed hat pulled down over his eyes. Lesech drove the 60-odd kilometres to Paris without encountering a German patrol. There was only one moment's anxiety at the Porte de Clichy, where, just for once, he presented the check-point commander with a bottle of Calvados. The MP sergeant came over and peered at the passenger on the front seat, but Lesech got in first — 'He's sleeping it off, had a drop too much' — and quickly drove on.

And the end of the story?

Abbé Jeglot, my friend and associate from the Église de la Trinité, came to the rescue once more. By arrangement with a family whose son was wanted by the German police and had fled to the provinces, the body was taken to their house. A friendly Resistance doctor made out a death certificate in the son's name and Abbé Jeglot conducted the funeral service at his church, thereby killing two birds with one stone: the agent's body had been disposed of and the young man, officially dead and buried, was deleted from the Germans' 'Wanted' list.

* * *

Heedless of my existing work-load, London now burdened me with two more tasks. One was to keep various Resistance networks supplied with funds dispatched from England, the other to establish contact with agents whose cover had been blown, take them under my wing and convey them to safety across the Channel. This latter activity was exceptionally dangerous because I might well be exposing myself to a network infiltrated by agents of the Gestapo or the Abwehr (German military counter-intelligence). This, in fact, was the cause of my misfortunes a few months later.

My network's 'passengers' were growing in number. Eleven had already crossed the Pyrenees or got to England by Lysander. I now had two sites suitable for air drops and Lysander landings at La Ferté and Rugies.

⋆ ⋆ ⋆

Christmas, 1943, was ten days off. London had transmitted a message instructing me to take personal delivery of a suitcase to be landed by Lysander that night, its contents being cash destined for two Resistance organizations in Paris. The operation went without a hitch. Two new arrivals were dropped at Créteil, where they left us and continued on their way. I myself escorted the suitcase, together with a third agent from England, to one of my hide-outs near Porte de Vincennes, the home of the Loire family.

Victor Loire, a man of retirement age, used to provide me with a safe-house when need arose. He and his wife kept a room permanently at my disposal in their small apartment at No. 8, rue Fernand-Foureau, and this was where I opened the suitcase, which contained nearly three million francs in used notes of various denominations. Having divided up the cash in accordance with my instructions, I entrusted the smaller sum to one of my couriers, Fernand Carlier, alias

Cristin. I myself took charge of the remaining two-and-a-half million francs, which had to be delivered to Avenue de La Bourdonnais, near Les Invalides. The safest plan was to take the Métro via the Gare de Lyon. So many passengers converged on or left the main-line station carrying suitcases that the fact that I had one with me would seem quite unexceptional.

Hans

Police checks at the Gare de Lyon were conducted sometimes inside the station itself and sometimes in the Métro ticket hall. There was little risk of being intercepted as I mingled with the crowd on the platform, waiting for the next train. The train that followed the one from which I had alighted was almost empty. I got in and sat down in my favourite spot, just inside the doors with my back to them. This had the advantage of enabling me to make a rapid exit if necessary.

Two young Wehrmacht NCOs followed me in, accompanied by a couple of

French girls whom they had obviously picked up in some neighbouring bar. They looked somewhat the worse for wear — surprisingly so, because tipsy German soldiers were seldom seen in public. Evidently on leave in 'gay Paree', they wanted to cut a dash with their *Mamsellen*.

To lessen the chances of being recognized while out on certain missions, I sometimes sported a broad-brimmed felt hat and a long trenchcoat *à la* Gestapo. In their eagerness to impress the girls, the two soldiers devised a way of amusing them. I heard them announce that they proposed to bait 'that funny-looking *Franzose* with his hat over his ears', and, if he lost his wool and swore at them, hand him over to the *Kettenhunde* (slang for military police) at the next stop. For me, who would have found it hard to explain all the banknotes in my suitcase, this boded no good at all.

An elbow jabbed me in the ribs and a hand tipped the hat over my eyes. I straightened it, but the procedure was repeated three or four times. The girls roared with laughter. What to do? I would have to react soon, or my tormentors would dream up some other idea. Knowing the German habit of obedience, I decided to trade on it. Besides, I could see that neither man was wearing SS insignia.

Without rising from my seat, I turned and barked at them. 'You two, come here at once and show me your paybooks.' They stared at me in surprise. '*Er spricht Deutsch*,' said one of them. 'Haven't you ever seen a Frenchman in the service of the Third Reich?' I continued in the same tone of voice. Obediently, they handed over their *Soldbücher*, which I promptly pocketed. 'But . . . ' protested one of them, who was wearing the Iron Cross. 'Silence!' I snapped. 'You can retrieve your paybooks from General von Stülpnagel at the Kommandantur tomorrow morning. You'll have less to laugh about then, believe me!' We pulled into another station. The Germans and their girlfriends had lapsed into silence and were looking thoroughly deflated. I myself was feeling better. My bluff had worked, but I would have to put an end to the situation in short order.

I took the paybooks from my pocket and leafed slowly through them while the Germans watched me apprehensively. I learned that the one who was wearing the Iron Cross had won it for gallantry in action outside Leningrad, and that his first name was Hans.

'Hans, come here,' I said in a milder tone. 'Don't be a fool. Why spoil a nice leave in Paris — a well-earned one, to judge by your record — for the sake of two tarts who are only after your money? Do you want to be sent back to the eastern Front? I'll overlook your behaviour this time, but you must do as I say. Get out at the next station and leave the girls with me. I'll see they're handed over to the vice squad. Here are your paybooks. Now get lost. I did some daft things myself at your age. You can thank your lucky stars I'm an understanding man.'

They left the train without a word, just clicked their heels and gave me a Hitler salute. Their eyes were brimming with tears of gratitude!

I ejected one of the girls a few stations further along the line and the other a little later. Having long ago passed my destination, I remained aboard. At the terminus I got out and made for the nearest café, where I sank two large brandies to steady my nerves. My knees were still trembling with fright.

Catching a train in the opposite direction, I delivered the suitcase to Avenue de La Bourdonnais without further incident.

'Frau Goering'

Between Christmas and the New Year, 1943, I had to go to Marseilles to settle certain matters relating to exfiltrations by the southern sector of my network. I took advantage of the occasion, as I have already said, to spend a few relaxing days with the Reynauds, the close friends who had sheltered me in 1940.

The journey passed off without incident, but the train was very late as usual and the curfew had already been in force for some time. On such occasions passengers were obliged to spend the night in station waiting-rooms, where their identity cards, travel permits and luggage were carefully scrutinized. I had to avoid this at all costs, because although my papers were covered with the requisite official stamps and would have withstood a routine check, they were, of course, forgeries.

German passengers and military personnel were entitled to leave the station through a separate gateway guarded by members of the *Feldpolizei*. Encouraged by my successful bluff in the Paris Métro, I mingled with a group of Germans and strode firmly towards the exit with my head held high.

'*Wo wollen Sie hin?*' the sentry demanded. I knew from previous experience which Marseilles hotel housed the Gestapo's junior officers and their French henchmen, and my papers included a permit bearing the stamp of the Lille SD. 'The Hôtel Splendide,' I replied. 'Untersturmführer Witke is expecting me. I don't know Marseilles, can you tell me which way to go?' The sentry ignored this. 'What's in that bag of yours?' he asked. He was an amiable-looking man of a certain age, and I estimated that a jocular response might do the trick. 'Frau Goering,' I replied, lowering my voice confidentially. 'I've brought my friend the Untersturmführer a nice, fat goose. We're going to have a Christmas dinner fit for a king.' The sentry laughed heartily at my quip and directed me to the Hôtel Splendide, whose location was only too familiar to me.

Hugging the walls with eyes peeled and ears pricked for German patrols, I made my way to the Reynauds'. It was after midnight when I rang their bell, to be welcomed all the more warmly because they'd given up hope of seeing me at so late an hour.

Madame Goering was a great success. Cooking her on a stove over smouldering sawdust, the only fuel available, was a lengthy business that left her charred on the outside and raw within, but we devoured her with gusto. It was a long time since the household had enjoyed such a meal, which made a pleasant change from boiled swedes or the meatless wartime dish ironically referred to as *gigot Pétain* (thick-sliced aubergines rolled in wholemeal flour and fried in ersatz oil).

★ ★ ★

In January, 1944, I made two more trips to Belgium and Holland, where I extended the network to Delfzyl, a small fishing port in the north of Groningen province, not far from the German frontier. There, at the terminus of the SOE's Danish pipeline, I met Per Jensen, a local fisherman and *passeur* for agents from Denmark. On the way back I got in touch at Harlingen with a family named Fonteyn, who were later to run an efficient safe-house there.

Then it was south once more to visit Mirande in Gers and a maquis unit based near Murat. Ideally situated only an hour's bus-ride north of Tarbes, Mirande was a perfect place for 'passengers' to wait before crossing into Spain. A small, secluded town of less than 3,000 inhabitants, it seldom if ever saw a German. A member of my network had some distant relations who lived there and willingly acted as a safe-house. I don't know how often he used it because I failed to trace the courageous old couple after the war. Refugees from the north, they had taken a farmhouse near the town but returned to Cambrai, their place of origin, when the war ended.

As for the maquis of Murat, I had been informed that it was based near the Plomb du Cantal, the mountain overlooking the town, and felt that it might provide a suitable hideaway for network members who were in danger but unwilling to leave France and their families.

The maquis was controlled by the communist-dominated FTP (*Franc-Tireurs et Partisans*). Getting in touch with its trigger-happy members was a laborious and somewhat perilous business. Indeed, my contact at Murat had difficulty in persuading their commander to see me at all because his fear of *agents provocateurs* verged on the pathological. Blindfolded and covered with sacks of straw, I was conveyed to his headquarters in a farm cart, then closely questioned and harshly rebuked for failing to keep him supplied by air.

After much talk the tension eased and I promised the maquis chieftain an air drop of four containers of small arms.

In return he agreed to shelter members of my network and house their families in and around Murat, but not, under any circumstances, at his own or his friends' expense: the price of a week's board and lodging had to be agreed in advance. Although taken aback by the mercenary considerations to which these self-styled patriots attached such importance, I kept my word. In February, 1944, the RAF carried out an air drop in accordance with coordinates, codes and signals radioed to London by me.

★ ★ ★

By the time I had completed this 'Tour de France' by making supervisory visits to Cassis, Douvaine, the Swiss frontier and Dijon, I was utterly exhausted — swallowing amphetamines and black coffee to stay awake, then sedatives to snatch a few hours' sleep. It was high time I took a rest, but the network's increasing activity precluded me from any such self-indulgence. Jacques had solved the problem of radio transmissions from the South of France, and it urgently behoved me to do the same for the Belgian and Dutch section of the network. Sadly, I never got the chance.

Although I seldom attended air drops or Lysander landings in person, I was instructed by London to take delivery at Rugies of a substantial consignment of cash destined for various networks including my own. We landed two agents and dispatched twice that number in a turn-round time of less than seven minutes. As usual the new arrivals were taken to a safe-house in Paris to rest and relax. From there they proceeded under their own steam. Their final destinations were never divulged — it was better not to know — and their names were temporary pseudonyms.

Prelude to Disaster

In the middle of March, 1944, I received orders from London to contact 'Julien', an agent who had been blown and taken refuge in Paris. He was to be exfiltrated from France at the earliest opportunity. I had no Lysander landing in prospect, so he would have to use the Spanish route.

This type of operation had by now become routine and the initial contact was made without difficulty by a Parisian courier code-named Germaine. The rendezvous was the Tao Bar in rue Gaillon, near the Avenue de l'Opéra. Germaine should by rights have picked up her 'passenger' there the next day and taken him to a safe-house to wait, but fate decreed otherwise. What followed was entirely my own fault.

When she got home that night Germaine discovered that her little girl was ill, so she could not keep the next day's appointment. Was I overtired? Did I have too much on my mind? Whatever the reason, I neglected to send someone in Germaine's place. Her potential replacement was in luck — I wasn't, because, against all the rules, I decided to turn up at the rendezvous myself.

It was nearly midday when I entered the Tao Bar. Small shaded lamps on the tables bathed the interior in a subdued glow. There was a long bar on the left of the entrance, and the sofas and armchairs around the walls looked inviting. Although the place made an opulent impression, I had a strangely apprehensive feeling in the pit of my stomach. I went up to the bar and asked if Julien had arrived. 'No, not yet,' I was told, 'but he won't be long. He phoned a few minutes ago.' It was precisely the reply I'd been expecting. Faintly reassured, I ordered a Pernod. A girl sat down beside me, a hostess from the look of her. I bought her a daiquiri and engaged her in conversation, that being the natural thing to do in such an establishment if I didn't want to draw attention to myself. Then I got a shock: 'Take care,' she told me in a low voice, 'it's a trap.'

I half-turned with one hand on her thigh, gently squeezing it to convey that I'd got the message. Hovering near the door was a ferrety-faced man who looked out of place in such surroundings. Another two equally unprepossessing individuals were seated at a table in the far corner. I went to the *toilettes* in the hope of finding another exit. One of the duo rose at once and followed me, evidently to see if I would try to conceal something.

When I returned the barman told me that Julien had arrived and pointed out the table where he was sitting. I noticed, however, that he nodded almost imperceptibly to the man near the door, who sauntered out.

That settled it. Realizing that I was indeed in a trap, I knew I must concoct a plausible story for Julien to relay to my future interrogators, as he undoubtedly would, and put them off the scent. Unaware that they had caught the head of a network, they probably assumed that I was a leg-man who might lead them to his boss. My brain worked overtime as I ran through all the tricks that had been taught me in training.

13

A Prisoner of the Germans

WHEN I left my flat to keep the appointment with Julien some sixth sense had prompted me to carry, as I sometimes did, the set of papers identifying me as Pierre Lalande of rue de la Pompe. They had been fabricated in London and were complete forgeries, but they would offer no lead to an investigator. My keys were my only Achilles' heel. While giving a banknote to the hostess, whom I knew to be on my side because she had alerted me, I slipped them into her hand. She caught on at once and surreptitiously dropped them into her handbag. I never knew her name, but it was yet another demonstration that girls like her, whose trade obliged them to consort with the enemy, could often be staunch patriots.

I went over to Julien's table and sat down. He proceeded to tell me, in a wealth of detail far too elaborate to be authentic, how he had been hunted by the Gestapo as a member of a network based at Charleville in the French Ardennes. He even gave me the names of his superiors and bragged about the operations he had taken part in. His aim was to reassure me and encourage me to open up in my turn.

Which was what I did, except that my story hailed from the realms of pure invention. I told him that I came from Arras and had gone underground to avoid being sent to Germany with the compulsory labour service. I lived by dabbling in the black market. An acquaintance named Bastien, another black marketeer whom I occasionally bumped into at a bar we both frequented, had asked me that morning if I would do him a favour: Would I meet Julien at the Tao Bar and tell him to rendezvous with Bastien at the left luggage counter in the Gare Saint-Lazare, where he had to deposit some parcels. He was to be there on the stroke of five-fifteen and identify himself by blowing his nose three times on a pink handkerchief.

I chuckled inwardly at the thought of this traitor combing Paris for a snotrag of the stipulated colour. My nerves were on edge and it soothed me to see the funny side of the situation. Knowing that everything might depend on this preliminary exchange, I had to score a bull's-eye the very first time.

Procrastination was a textbook tactic, so I adopted it and invited Julien to have a Pernod. I stood myself one too, aware that it might be my last. Sipping it slowly, I proceeded to sow another seed in my opponent's mind, namely that I had nothing in common with those 'communist gangsters' in the FTP. This I did because I knew what fate the Gestapo reserved for members of that communist-dominated organization. I described how, over a year earlier, a vague acquaintance from my school days had invited me to join one of their Resistance cells. Having witnessed the methods employed by the 'cocos' in 1936, when the Popular Front was rampant, I had preserved an ingrained hatred of them and declined his invitation.

That set the stage for the performance

to come. Clearly disconcerted by my remarks, Julien rose and took his leave, but not before asking me why, if I detested the communists so much, I hadn't joined the Milice, Pétain's Vichy militia. I dodged the question. A few minutes later I paid up and left, promptly followed by the two unsavoury types in the corner.

The girl was still at the bar when I made my exit. Glancing over my shoulder, I saw her surreptitiously cross herself.

There might still, I thought, be a chance of losing my two shadows in the subterranean passages of the Place de l'Opéra Métro station. No such luck. Fifty metres away I saw two black Citroëns parked beside the kerb. I couldn't turn back; the two men — German police, as I later discovered — were barring my path. The car doors opened and more men emerged. They thrust me into a doorway and handcuffed me. Then, hemmed in on all sides, I was hustled into the leading car.

The passers-by had noticed nothing — either that, or they turned a blind eye. Such incidents were a daily spectacle in occupied Paris.

Julien had got in beside the driver while I sat sandwiched between two plainclothesmen, one of them being the ferret-face from the Tao Bar. I now knew for sure which way the wind blew and was glad to have been able to spin my yarn to Julien.

Only one question preyed on my mind: Who were my captors? The Gestapo? The Milice from rue Lauriston? Or the Abwehr from Avenue Foch? I dreaded the first two, who were notorious for their brutal interrogation methods. Abwehr personnel, by contrast, were professional soldiers who tended to treat their prisoners like human beings. My question was answered when we rounded the Arc de Triomphe and drove down the Avenue Foch. I breathed easier in the knowledge that my captors did not belong to either of the first two categories.

The date was 20 March, 1944. A new chapter in my life had begun. I couldn't help wondering if it would be the last.

We ascended the marble stairs of the former Rothschild mansion, where I was handcuffed to a radiator in a kind of pantry. It had a little service lift that probably led to the kitchens in the basement, but there was no way I could free myself and attempt to escape.

A soldier came in and searched me. He removed my wallet, tie and shoes, but left me my watch. The minutes dragged by. I sat there on the flagstones with one arm in the air, my wrist cuffed to the top of the radiator. Having long ago acquired the knack of dozing off whenever an opportunity presented itself, I recouped my energies by snatching some sleep.

'*Aufstehen!*' The sergeant who had barked out the word, jolting me awake, was followed into the room by a colonel whose army insignia confirmed that I was indeed a prisoner of the Abwehr, not the Gestapo. He eyed me closely. Then, unaware that I spoke German, he said, 'This isn't the man we're after.' I was delighted, because now I could build on my story accordingly. 'You go to the station and pick up this Bastien fellow,' he told the sergeant. 'Julien will tell you how to recognize him. Report to me as soon as you get back.' The colonel indicated me. 'He's of minor interest.'

It was hard to suppress a look of jubilation. The yarn I'd spun Julien had been swallowed, hook, line and sinker. I discovered later that the colonel was Oberst Riele, head of the Paris Abwehr. The sergeant I often saw again. He was Hugo Bleicher, who became my *Sachbearbeiter*, the case officer responsible for interrogating me.

The door closed behind them. Night had fallen and it was too dark to see the time by my watch. I was hungry, not having eaten anything since early that morning. I fell asleep again, still with one arm in the air, though my wrist was becoming painful because of the handcuff constricting it.

The light came on. I opened my eyes, blinking, to see Bleicher and a private soldier standing over me. The soldier urged me to my feet by prodding me in the back with his rifle-butt.

'*Das war nur Quatsch, was Sie Julien erzählt haben,*' (It was all nonsense, what you told Julien). Then, in broken French, 'come with us.' The soldier detached my wrist from the radiator and I was allowed to retrieve my shoes, which had been tossed into a corner. Then I was taken to the floor above. While climbing the stairs I spotted a large number of air-drop containers on the landings below and wondered how they had got there.

Another mystery awaited me in the guardroom, where some Romanian SS men were having supper. It contained an oil painting of a British officer who might have been General Gubbins's twin. Going over to it, I saw that it was signed 'John Starr'. The Romanians inquired in sign language if I had eaten. When I shook my head they gave me a plateful of chick-peas with a piece of sausage on top — even a glass of beer. The soldiers were considerate and the food did me good. Formerly servants' quarters, the rooms on this top floor had been partitioned off into cells, of which I seemed at present to be the only occupant. I was given two blankets and enjoyed a good night's rest on my bunk bed.

It wasn't until the following afternoon that I was taken back downstairs to the floor below, where Bleicher was waiting for me. He was wearing civilian clothes and accompanied by a Frenchman, evidently an interpreter.

Having retained a certain singsong intonation from my boyhood in French-speaking Switzerland, not to mention one or two Belgicisms from my later years, I was afraid that these peculiarities might become apparent under pressure and invalidate the story I proposed to tell. I quickly decided to answer the sergeant's opening questions in German.

'*Sie sprechen also doch Deutsch!*' said Bleicher, delighted to be able to dispense with an interpreter.

On the spur of the moment I admitted that my papers were false. Bastien had procured them for me to cover my black market operations. My real name was André Bérard. I was a native of Arras and lived in Boulevard Péreire. It was safe enough for me to reveal the address. The apartment contained nothing incriminating and I had taken it over from a big shot in the Gestapo, an excellent piece of 'décor'! Madame Tourraine never came to clean it unless I myself was present. As for Maryse, who was the only other person to visit or phone me there, she thought me a black marketeer in any case, so that trail would lead nowhere.

Bleicher went over to the attack. '*Aber der Bastien war nicht am Bahnhof!*' I registered amusement. Of course Bastien hadn't shown up, I replied. When he failed to see a sign of me he must have smelt a rat and cleared off — routine practice for a black marketeer. Whoever had stopped me going to the station was a fool, I went on, meaning the colonel. I'd scored my first point: Bleicher was clearly annoyed with his boss.

I was asked to give a description of Bastien and shown some photographs. Among them was a picture of the man who had followed me into the washroom at the Tao Bar. I pointed to it. Bleicher at first looked taken aback that I should have picked out one of his own operatives, but I gathered from his fleeting grin that he'd seen the joke.

There was a commotion on the landing. Bleicher went out to investigate and returned smiling broadly. '*Wir haben einen großen Fisch gefangen!*' he said, and told me that he couldn't spare any more time to question me today. My reassuring conclusion: if he was so pleased about the big fish they'd caught, I must be a very small one.

I was escorted back to my cell on the top floor, but not for long. Handcuffed once more, this time with my arms behind my back, I was driven to the Santé Prison in one of the inevitable black Citroën saloons and there transferred to a prison van. I could hear more prisoners being thrust into the other cells in that grim vehicle. We drove for what seemed like hours, then came to a halt.

Our destination turned out to be Fresnes Prison, and Fresnes was no holiday resort. I and a handful of others were prodded inside with rifle butts and ordered to line up. When our names were called, one by one, we made our way into a long room. My turn came. 'Bérard!' At least Bleicher had accepted the second false identity I'd given him. We were booked in, photographed, and told to remove all our clothes, which the guards carefully inspected for concealed files or other prohibited objects.

Stark naked, we were herded into the

showers to the accompaniment of more digs in the back. It seemed that we 'Sauen', or pigs, needed a wash. We were then permitted to get dressed and told to roll up our sleeves and trouser-legs. We didn't do this quickly enough to suit our guards. Another hail of blows descended on us, and I received a kick in the buttocks while standing on one leg to pull up my trousers. Needless to say, I fell to my knees. It was a performance designed to intimidate.

We were marched along endless corridors and split up. I saw a sign: '3ème Division.' Here our escorts left us and handed me over to an Obergefreiter (corporal) who must have passed the normal age of retirement. Using sign language and the little French he knew, he informed me that he was in charge of my floor and that I had to salute him. He was clearly relieved when I answered him in German, and said it would make things simpler.

My new quarters were Cell 214. The heavy door opened and shut behind me with a muffled thud. I inspected the premises. The latrine, situated in the corner nearest the door, was a stinking hole in the floor *à la turque*. The cell contained a folding bunk and a shelf but no chair. It was dimly lit by a naked bulb high up near the ceiling.

I no longer had my watch, but it must have been about 8 p.m. I was hungry, having eaten nothing all day but a hunk of dry bread. There was no form of heating and the late March evening was chilly. I lowered the bunk and wrapped myself as best I could in the one thin blanket, which smelt as mouldy as the mattress. Cell 214 was certainly no five star hotel, but I tried to sleep despite my discomfort and the innumerable thoughts that were coursing through my brain. This was my second day in captivity. If 'they' had made some major discovery I would have been questioned about it at once, so my network must still be intact. I had set the stage for the performance I would have to give in order to preserve it from destruction.

To stay alive I would have to court interrogation and spin out the sessions for as long as possible, thereby postponing my 'trial', whose outcome would certainly not be favourable. My covert activities had acquainted me with a great deal of information about agents and *résistants* who had left the shores of France and were no longer at risk. It should be possible to select outdated and unimportant details and feed them to my interrogators one by one. The time they took to assimilate and check them could only work to my advantage. What was more, if I were interrogated in German and pretended not to understand the language too well, I should be able to gain time by asking for questions to be repeated. I could also give deliberately evasive replies without arousing suspicion. One ominous possibility: I knew that the Abwehr was sometimes obliged to 'lend' its prisoners to the Gestapo for questioning, and the Gestapo's methods were considerably more brutal.

I awoke with a start. Shouts, the rattle of mess tins, doors opening and shutting. It was 4.30 a.m., as I discovered when my own door opened. '*Aufstehen!*' I had to stand to attention in the doorway. I could see other prisoners drawn up in the same position with mugs at the ready. I earned my first tongue-lashing by pointing out that my cell was not equipped with a mug. This deprived me of my ration of the brownish liquid, derisorily referred to as coffee, which a fellow detainee was pushing along in a big drum on wheels. The soldier escorting him distributed hunks of bread. Even the pail for sluicing the latrine was empty, so I resigned myself to eating mine dry.

I returned quietly to my bunk and lay down again. This earned me a second reprimand when the corporal appeared with a mug and a mess tin. It was '*strengstens verboten*' to go back to bed after 'breakfast': bunks had to be made and folded back against the wall. I was also issued with a small broom from which a few bristles still protruded and told to clean my cell, sweeping the dust into a corner near the door. At 9 a.m. the dust would be removed and my pail replenished. The corporal wanted to see the floor 'shine' when he came to inspect it later on. How was I to achieve this? By 'boning' it with the broom-head, and woe betide me if I failed. The contents of the pail would be emptied over the floor, obliging me to start again from scratch.

It was a very effective way of breaking a prisoner's spirit. On the other hand, the exercise helped to combat the all-pervading chill.

Today was exercise day, which meant that we circled a dismal concrete yard in groups of twenty, forbidden to speak. From time to time the order '*Im Laufschritt!*' rang out, and we obediently broke into a double. Twenty minutes of this, and we were marched back to our cells. I noticed that, like one or two others on the same floor, my door bore a red card inscribed 'GEFÄHRLICH — STÄNDIG KONTROLLIEREN' (Dangerous — Constant Supervision).

This was something new for me to worry about, but another day had gone by. I tried to be calm and philosophical. While there was life there was hope.

At coffee time next morning I was handed a razor and a small piece of broken mirror glass and told to spruce myself up. I hadn't shaved for three days, there was no soap, and the blade had already seen a lot of service. The result was excruciating. '*Tribunal*,' the corporal announced. This was the word that always prefaced a trip to Paris for interrogation, either by the Abwehr or by the dreaded Gestapo, but I didn't discover that until later. I was outwardly calm but inwardly uneasy.

Bleicher, who was waiting for me at the Avenue Foch, seemed to be in a very bad mood. Seated in his office was a man in SS uniform, Sonderführer (civilian supernumerary of officer status) Ernst Vogt. I was handcuffed once more and bundled into a Citroën saloon with blacked-out side and rear windows. I had no idea where they were taking me and was no wiser when we got there. The car pulled up in an enclosed courtyard and a guard hauled me out.

With the guard's machine pistol prodding me in the back, I was marched up some stairs and along a succession of passages. There were SS men everywhere. The interview room was empty save for the chair in which Vogt sat, the table in front of it, and a photoportrait of Hitler on the wall. The Führer, with toothbrush moustache and drooping lock of hair, seemed to be regarding me malignly.

A senior SS officer came in. I knew his face, having seen pictures of it in the paper. He was Obersturmbannführer (Lieutenant-Colonel) Kieffer, the SD's number one in Paris. 'Who is this fellow?' he asked Vogt in German, looking me up and down. 'Only a little fish,' Vogt replied, 'but he may know something. If he does, we'll get it out of him.' Vogt also assumed that I didn't understand German. I decided not to disabuse him.

The day's entertainment was prefaced by some hard slaps across the face from two of Vogt's sidekicks, who were stationed behind me. 'You're a terrorist! You'll be shot if you go on lying!' Vogt consulted the notes given him by Bleicher, which were lying on the table in front of him. I had to repeat my story point by point. He tried in vain to get me to modify it and diverge, however slightly, from the statements I'd made to Julien at the Tao Bar and Bleicher at the Avenue Foch.

When I stuck to my guns in spite of the blows that rained down on my head and every part of my body, Vogt lost his temper. 'Think you're tough, do you? Very well, we have other methods of persuasion!'

This heralded my first acquaintance with the 'bath-tub' interrogation technique. My head was immersed in cold water again and again and held there until I thought my lungs would burst. 'I only want to tell you the truth,' I gasped when I got my breath back. 'So let's hear it,' said Vogt. Stripped naked and shivering with cold, I repeated what I had already told him, word for word. Another ducking session followed, and another. I wondered how much longer I would be able to hold out.

I had been taught in England how to fake a fit of hysteria. I rolled on the floor and lashed out with my arms and legs, yelling inarticulately. The SS men's hail of blows, which were meant to silence me, had the desired effect: I genuinely passed out.

A glass of cognac brought me round and the guards chafed my limbs to restore the circulation. Vogt offered me a cigarette. I went down on my knees, my voice racked with sobs. 'It's no use telling lies just to please you, you'd be bound to find out in the end. Have a heart, can't you? I didn't do anything really bad. I thought it was just to do with the black market.'

Vogt turned to his henchmen. 'I reckon he's telling the truth,' he said in German. 'That man Bleicher can tie up the loose ends.' His tone of voice was eloquent of the SD's contempt for the Abwehr. 'Take him away!'

Covered in bruises but happy to have passed the test, I got back to Fresnes too late for the evening soup ration. My corporal, whose name I now knew was Albrecht, wagged his head at the sight of my swollen face. He obviously had no love for the SS, because he muttered, 'They're animals, those people, not human beings. Me, I'm a German soldier.' As if to demonstrate what he meant, he fetched his vacuum flask and filled my mess-tin with some hot soup that certainly hadn't emanated from the prison kitchens. A PoW in France during the 1914 – 18 war, Albrecht had spent some time working on a farm there. He had always been well treated and the memory lingered on.

Another week went by. My SD interrogation made me realize how close I had come to disclosing information of value. It was time to revise my Harley Street lessons on self-induced oblivion and put them into practice.

I pretended to be suffering from violent headaches brought on by the beating I had received. Albrecht sent me to the infirmary where I was given some aspirins and granted permission to remain lying down in my cell for a week. This spell of repose, together with the relative silence that reigned in the prison, enabled me to concentrate on 'cleansing' my memory. I was assisted in this process, in which all thoughts of the past had to be banished from my mind, by another form of activity.

For some days I had been scratching myself like a maniac, tormented by an infestation of fleas that left itchy red spots all over my body. I decided to make use of the creatures. Training them would be a task requiring patience and concentration. I began by making them jump a wisp of straw from my palliasse. Then came more complicated evolutions, like getting them to walk the tightrope on a piece of string. They were extraordinarily intelligent and never came a cropper even when I altered the length of a jump at the very last moment.

Early one morning the razor made its reappearance. '*Sie müssen sich leider fürs Tribunal wieder fertigmachen,*' Albrecht told me regretfully. I was to get ready for another grilling, but I felt confident that my exercises in autosuggestion would have wiped the network's vulnerable points from my memory.

The police van pulled up outside the Gestapo building in Place Beauvau, as before. Things got off to a bad start. Showered with blows as soon as I emerged, I was frogmarched to a grimy room where a new inquisitor was awaiting me: an SS man with eyes like a toad, greasy hair and black-rimmed nails. The uniform trousers that enveloped his short legs and ample posterior were covered with stains and hadn't seen an iron for weeks.

His opening words — '*Wieder ein kommunistischer Gauner!* (Another communist scoundrel)' — said it all: he was solely interested in knowing whether or not I belonged to the FTP.

I had no chance to reply. Two SS men hurled me to the floor and reduced my face to raw meat with their boots, knocking out two teeth in the first few moments. My ribs, of which at least one was broken, hurt like hell. Lying sprawled near the door, which was ajar, I grasped it and tried to haul myself to my feet. One of the SS men kicked it shut, crushing my middle finger. I stared stupidly at the wobbly joint in which it now terminated.

After the hors-d'oeuvres came the main course. My inquisitor, whose name I never discovered, asked me the same old questions. He, too, had some notes at which he peered short-sightedly from time to time. Knowing the subject that interested him most, I framed my replies accordingly. Bastien, 'a dangerous terrorist', was the man he was trying to nail, and Bastien was just a figment of my imagination! I built on what I had told Julien at the Tao Bar and embroidered my story still further. The Popular Front years had left their mark on me. My loathing of the communists and their socialist confederates had prompted me to join the right-wing paramilitary organization headed by Colonel de la Roque. When asked to participate in a political assassination, however, I had balked and resigned my membership. I had a horror of the sight of blood, which was my main reason for going underground when mobilization was proclaimed. I was just a cowardly individual who had severed all ties with his family and friends and now scraped a living on the black market.

I was given another going-over, then told that I would be sent off to work in Germany: there, at least, I would be of some service to the anti-communist cause. My interrogation had lasted less than an hour and a half. On the strength of my statements, which confirmed what he had already learned from Vogt and Bleicher, my inquisitor clearly thought it unnecessary to waste any more time on me.

A Gestapo car drove me to Santé

Prison to await the police van that would take me back to Fresnes. Together with a mixed bunch of prisoners, old and new, I was temporarily confined in the 'cage' that had formerly been used as overnight accommodation for prostitutes charged with soliciting. I must have been an unattractive sight, with my torn shirt, black eye, split lip and eyebrow, bloody face and missing teeth. I could read fear of what lay ahead in the eyes of those who, for the first time, found themselves in the clutches of the German authorities.

It was still early when I returned to Fresnes. Albrecht, solicitous as ever, escorted me to the infirmary where they strapped up my broken ribs and smeared my cuts and abrasions with ointment. I was also given three stitches, one in the lip and two in the eyebrow, and a couple of aspirin tablets. I still don't know how I managed to sleep that night.

The prospect of doing forced labour in Germany didn't appeal to me. I had heard tell of prison factories from which no one returned alive, so I decided to delay my departure from Fresnes at all costs. The day of our release could not be far off. Rumour had it that the German Army was being decimated on the Italian and Russian fronts and would soon collapse. News travelled between the prison's various floors via the latrine holes, an effective if malodorous method of communication.

Easter came and went. Bleicher paid a visit to the infirmary to interrogate a detainee too sick to be moved. He had obviously taken advantage of the occasion to issue Albrecht with special instructions, because the elderly corporal was more than usually affable. Pointing to my face, which was still puffy and discoloured, he treated me to what was, for him, a lengthy speech. 'The others,' he said, meaning the SD and Gestapo, 'are also convinced you're telling the truth. I have a suggestion for you: Why not co-operate with us? After all, the communists are your enemies as well as ours. Think it over, otherwise you'll be shipped off to Germany.'

It was an overt and well-meant invitation on his part. Guessing that anything I said would be faithfully reported to Bleicher, I came out with a 'revelation': I had, in fact, worked for Bastien as a paid courier. I had no faith in the SD and the Gestapo, who had maltreated me, so I wouldn't confide in anyone but Bleicher and his Abwehr officers, who were soldiers, not sadists.

Albrecht was delighted by my response to his proposal, which would doubtless earn him a spell of long-awaited leave. He congratulated me on my decision. According to him, I would probably have to atone for my black-marketeering by spending another two or three months in prison and then be released.

Our conversation soon bore fruit. Five days later I was recalled to the Avenue Foch, a comedy that repeated itself no less than seven times. On each occasion I fed Bleicher a titbit in the shape of some errand I had run for Bastien in my role as a courier. Although the incidents I described were authentic and verifiable, I knew that they presented no danger to anyone because the meeting places had long ago been abandoned and the persons concerned were safe from the attentions of the German police.

That was how I contrived to send Bleicher's sidekicks off on wild-goose chases the length and breadth of France. They returned empty-handed every time, satisfied that, although the birds had flown, my information was genuine.

Any doubts expressed by Bleicher were easily dispelled: Bastien would certainly have taken precautions as soon as I was arrested, and the fact that his men had failed to find anything proved as much. I suggested that it might be useful to take me along on these expeditions, reminding him of what had happened at the Gare Saint-Lazare. To that end I invented another story and 'revealed' that I had made several trips to Lyons to see a man named Jean Bart. On one occasion I had been instructed to hand him a small, locked suitcase. Bleicher asked me to describe it. My description fitted that of a transceiver.

Bleicher rose, rummaged in a cupboard, and produced a suit-case like the one I had described. I confirmed the resemblance. Bleicher beamed: 'This is a wireless transmitter. It was in a container parachuted into France by the British. We captured it!'

This time the fish was well and truly hooked. I was to travel to Lyons accompanied by Probst, one of Bleicher's colleagues, and a French informer named Maugenet. The pair were introduced to me and the arrangements for our trip, which was scheduled for a week hence, were worked out in detail. It was a delicate undertaking because the Abwehr could not afford to tread on the toes of the Lyons Gestapo, who were very touchy. I would meet 'Jean Bart' at the usual place, a café restaurant near Perrache station.

On one of my previous visits to Bleicher, which had ceased to be interrogations and resembled semi-friendly conversations, I had told him how bored I was in prison. I even described my flea training sessions, which made him laugh, and confessed to being an amateur poet, buttressing that assertion by reciting a poem by Schiller which I had learned at school. If only I had a pencil and paper, I sighed. Bleicher promptly scribbled a note for me to hand to Albrecht, with the result that a chair and some writing materials made their appearance in Cell 214. Two plus one plus four make seven, a number that has always been good to me. I was overjoyed!

While returning to Fresnes from Bleicher's office by car (no more prison vans for me!) I was struck by a sudden idea. On my trip to Lyons I would seize the opportunity to slip a coded message for Doris to one of the barmen in the station buffet, who was a Resistance sympathizer and had helped me in the past. He knew where my dead-letter-boxes were. I need only indicate which one to use by putting a numeral at the head of the message.

Next day, on the pretence of writing a poem, I drafted the message and concealed it in my straw mattress.

And then the worst happened: suspecting that one of the trusties in charge of soup distribution had slipped a weapon to a fellow prisoner, the prison authorities ordered a thorough search of every cell on my floor. It was conducted by a couple of SS guards while Albrecht, a mere spectator, looked on. My turn came. I was ordered to strip to my pants and remove my shoes. I knew that my palliasse would be ripped open and its contents strewn on the floor, so I sidled over to my bunk and sat down on it while the SS men were searching the rest of the cell. Pretending that the injury to my finger made it difficult for me to undo my laces, I used one hand to fumble with them while the other, concealed behind my back, extracted the telltale slip of paper from its hiding-place and stuffed it into my mouth. As bad luck would have it, I was spotted. One of the SS men seized a shoe and hit me over the head while the other tried to force my jaws open. It was a waste of time: I had already chewed and swallowed all but a tiny, illegible shred of paper that remained lodged between my teeth. The guards departed in high dudgeon. They were after more than a scrap of paper.

Albrecht gave me a reproachful look and said he would have to report the incident. He stomped out and closed the door behind him, leaving me to remake my palliasse and clear up the mess the guards had created.

Bleicher must have been informed,

because he came to see me the very next day. Why should I have concealed and then swallowed a piece of paper? I told him that I'd written an offensive poem about the Gestapo, and that I dreaded its discovery. The prison authorities would undoubtedly have passed it on to them, and I didn't relish the thought of another spell in their clutches. Bleicher, too, would have earned himself a black mark for letting me have the paper in the first place. My regard for him had made me want to spare him a reprimand.

I could tell from Bleicher's expression that he was quite disconcerted by my self-sacrificing effort to 'protect' him, and that I was back in his good books. Although his faith in me had been restored, however, he said he could not exempt me from any punishment imposed by the prison governor. He already knew what this would be: two weeks in solitary confinement. 'That'll upset my plans, because your Lyons trip will have to be postponed.'

Bleicher's boss, Oberst Reile, had insisted that I undergo a test before making the trip. No Citroën this time, no handcuffs either. Seated beside Bleicher in the back of a Mercedes saloon chauffeured by an army driver, I was taken to a private house in Avenue Montaigne, a smart street near the Champs-Élysées. The door was opened by a maidservant. This was a doctor's house, not a military establishment, and the apparatus in his consulting-room resembled an electrocardiograph. He wired me up to it with the aid of suction pads. The ensuing session lasted nearly two hours and was interrupted only once, when cups of real coffee and cigarettes were handed round. Bleicher offered me a choice between Player's Navy Cut and Caporals. Although I preferred English cigarettes, I avoided his little trap by plumping for the latter.

I was asked a multifarious series of questions relating to my past life, my hobbies, my tastes in art, my favourite sports and political opinions. I was expected to reply pat each time, without a trace of hesitation. Here again, I was saved by my now automatic pretence of not entirely understanding questions framed in German. Meanwhile, the doctor's gadget recorded my physio-logical reactions on strips on paper. '*Ein kalter Fisch*' (a cold fish) was his verdict before proceeding to the next test.

I had been told at Harley Street that, provided I had thoroughly 'washed' my memory and did not resist hypnosis, I would almost certainly disclose nothing but the story I had substituted for reality. The essential thing was to avoid panicking and relax. I don't remember what questions I was asked, but I could tell from Bleicher's expression, when I emerged from the torpor induced by the techniques he had used, that I hadn't given the game away.

When I asked him on the drive back to Fresnes if my trip to Lyons could now go ahead, he replied that the decision rested with his boss. He also disclosed that the person who had conducted the tests was Major von Wedel, a well-known German neurologist and hypnotist who had chosen to live in Paris to avoid the bombing.

That was my last contact with Bleicher, Avenue Foch, or any of the German counter-intelligence services in Paris.

After the war I found out why: the SD had won its little war against the Abwehr. Bleicher and many of his colleagues were transferred elsewhere, some of them to combat units on the eastern Front.

Back at Fresnes I was taken straight to 'the hole', or solitary. No more Albrecht, whose domain didn't extend that far. No daylight, no bed or blanket, wrists handcuffed behind me, only one meal a day. It seemed more like a year than a fortnight.

On 17 May, 1944, fifty-eight days after my arrest, I was marched back to my cell. Unaccustomed to daylight, my eyes ached and smarted. The chair and writing materials had disappeared, but not Albrecht. He entered my cell bearing a glass jar in one hand and a bunch of lilac in the other. '*Heute ist doch dein Geburtstag, nicht wahr?*'

It was true: today was my birthday and lilac blossom was a favourite of mine. As a child I'd always been allowed to cut some in our garden at home. '*Du warst dumm,*' Albrecht went on '*aber jetzt ist's vorüber.*' Yes, I'd been stupid, but it was over now. Released from solitary and welcomed back with flowers — a memorable day indeed! I was even privileged to shave off my two-week-old beard with a new blade. That night I got a double ration of soup.

The days crept monotonously by. Surprised and disappointed to receive no word from Bleicher, I had nothing to do but think. Even the fleas had lost their power to entertain me. I added fourteen days to the last date scratched on my wall and started the calendar afresh.

That was how I knew it was 6 June when the prison began to hum with activity. By standing on tiptoe on my windowsill I could see the roofs of the other blocks. Wooden platforms were being constructed there. Later in the day I saw that soldiers had manned the light anti-aircraft guns mounted on them. Quite clearly something exceptional had happened.

Around six that evening some new arrivals spread the word: the Allies had landed in Normandy! On every floor of every wing voices were raised in the *Marseillaise* and the FTP's marching song. We got no soup that night.

276

Although they were clearly thrown by the news, memories of the Dieppe fiasco convinced the Germans that the Allies would never gain a foothold.

With my ear glued to the latrine hole, I listened to the news as it spread like wildfire. Through a crack in my door, which I had enlarged with my fork, I could see guards running from cell to cell in a vain attempt to quell the rising tide of sound. Fuelled by the thought that the day of deliverance was near, the singing continued until the small hours.

That was the song, *Le Soleil levant*, in which voices from all over the prison joined before dawn each morning. Its strains accompanied those who, as daybreak approached, were carted off to Mont Valérien or some other remote spot, there to be executed by firing squad. The SS were emptying the prison of all those whose luck had run out, all who had been denied the right to defend themselves in court and condemned to die by a stroke of the pen. In the eyes of our oppressors 'terrorists' had no rights at all. I was filled with admiration for the courage of those who went to their death with their heads held high. I saw many of them depart in that way and wondered when my own turn would come.

The most fantastic rumours circulated. One day the Allies were already at the gates of Paris; the next they had been driven back into the sea. Albrecht alone remained realistic. Although he told me what the newspapers said, he could read between the lines sufficiently well to know that the Third Reich was retreating on every front and could not survive much longer. The enthusiasm born of Hitler's early victories had evaporated. Albrecht now realized what a pass his country had been brought to by the man in whom he had once believed. The atrocities committed by the SS, SD and Gestapo sickened him. While remaining, in his own words, a good soldier and a patriotic German, he tried to draw closer to me.

A new clear-out took place on the morning of 8 August, 1944. Some of the cell doors bearing ominous red cards were opened and I caught sight of an SOE agent whom I'd met while in training at Beaulieu. He was marched off with several other prisoners. I waited with a pounding heart for my own door to be flung open, but nothing happened. Had Albrecht protected me? Possibly, but he wouldn't answer my questions any more. He looked disconsolate and morose. Rumour had it that Paris would be declared an open city and that the Allies had called a halt before entering it. For some days now distant gunfire had been audible in the quiet of the night.

On 15 August we learned that the inmates of Fresnes were to be evacuated. '*Transport nach Deutschland*' Albrecht announced tersely. The war would soon be over, he added, and he was going home too. We surmised that the Germans intended to retain us for use as hostages when negotiating a ceasefire.

We were summoned from our cells in alphabetical order and lined up in the passage in two separate ranks, one against each wall, with an armed guard pacing up and down between them. I was in the smaller group. We were told we were to be released, but I didn't believe it; a glance at the fellow prisoners in my group told me that most of them came from cells adorned, like mine, with a red card. Taking advantage of a moment when the guard had his back turned, I darted across the passage and secreted myself in the other rank. Albrecht saw me but said nothing. I discovered much later that the prisoners in my group had been taken to Mont Valérien and shot.

I made myself as inconspicuous as possible and held my hand to my face as though suffering from toothache. Undetected, I marched off with the others and boarded one of the trucks that were waiting for us inside the main gate.

We were driven to the freight yard at Pantin, a north-eastern suburb of Paris. It was alive with SS men toting suitcases and bundles of all kinds. Our train, an immensely long one, stretched away in a gentle curve that enabled me to see what it comprised. I counted two locomotives, two freight cars, a sandbagged flatcar bristling with machine guns, three carriages, and thirty-odd cattle wagons with strong steel mesh over every potential exit. Bringing up the rear was another fortified flatcar like the first.

The inscription on the cattle wagons had been crossed out in chalk and replaced with the words '110 STÜCK'. It was an easy sum to do: $30 \times 110 = 3300$. In other words, 3300 prisoners were to be crammed into the wagons like sardines. In 1949, when a count was made of those who had returned, the result was 349. Ten men in a row, one alive, nine ghosts . . . I'm still haunted by that Dantesque vision to this day.

My current pseudonym, B for Bérard, assigned me to the leading cattle wagon. The delay that ensued before we pulled out of Pantin was far longer than the first phase of the journey. After less than three-quarters of an hour the train stopped at the mouth of a small tunnel and the doors were opened one by one. '*Alle raus!*' yelled the SS guards, lining up along the track with their machine guns enfilading the train. There was certainly no chance of escape at this stage.

'Bérard!' Albrecht materialized in front of me. It seemed that he had persuaded his bosses to appoint me interpreter. He explained that a bridge had been destroyed and that we would have to cross the Marne by the road bridge in order to join another train being assembled on the far side of the river. To signalize my temporary status I was made to wear an armband — a swastika armband no less!

Although I donned it without any feelings of joy, I felt that it might be an aid to damage limitation. Brandishing a megaphone, the SS officer in charge of the train warned his prisoners that any attempt to escape would be punished and that twenty of us would be shot for each such attempt, which was doomed to fail in any case.

The SS men's baggage, alias loot, had to be unloaded and carried for them, a back-breaking job allotted to the occupants of the second and third cattle wagons. I had to translate the relevant orders, then take up my post beside the bridge. I saw a road sign reading 'Nanteuil-Sacy', which at least told me where we were. For nearly three hours, thanks to the armband that served as my *laissez-passer*, I was free as a bird. The SS ignored me because

I was temporarily one of their own. I had plenty of chances to slip away as I walked beside the procession trudging along the track. Should I have escaped and condemned a score of my comrades to death? The war was nearly over and my value to the network minimal. There are circumstances in which an officer may be justified in sending his men to certain death, but I had no such excuse. The future was in God's hands. I saw one prisoner make a dash for it. He was gunned down, together with the five men nearest him.

I need hardly say that, once stripped of my armband and herded into the leading cattle wagon of the new train waiting for us on an embankment across the river, I did not receive the warmest of welcomes. There were two factions: some who had seen me wearing the brassard mistook me for an informer and were terrified of reprisals if anything happened to me; others spat in my face and thrust me into a corner, hurling abuse.

We stopped again the next morning, this time in the station at Châlons-sur-Marne. The signals stood at red,

283

doubtless thanks to the station-master, who had mobilized the local Red Cross team. They were forbidden to give us food and water, however. The SS not only drove them back but, just to leave those courageous folk a souvenir, made us empty our latrine buckets on to the platform — a prime example of Nazi humour.

For five days the train made its circuitous way across Alsace and Lorraine, stopping many times *en route* as railway-men of the 'Fer' network strove vainly to halt it for good. We trundled through Troyes twice and Nancy three times. Then came Saarbrücken and Germany. Thereafter we continued on our way without further interruption.

Weimar Station. Like visitors to a zoo, the passengers on the opposite platform stared at the haggard faces visible through the barbed wire and steel mesh that covered the apertures in the sides of our cattle wagons. An hour later we pulled into Buchenwald. Five days, two hunks of dry bread. We were already counting our dead.

14

Buchenwald

A HILL in the midst of a pine forest. Below us in the distance, the Weimar plain. Where pines gave way to beech trees, these had been scorched by the sun and were already taking on their autumn tints. It had been a very hot summer, and the weather was as warm as ever.

The train came to a halt, the doors of the first two wagons slid back. Stiff after our cramped journey all the way from Pantin, we piled out. Our legs gave way and we fell to our knees, exhausted, as if giving thanks for our deliverance from those stinking coffins on wheels.

The SS soon restored order in our ranks with a combination of yells, kicks and blows from their rifle butts. '*Im Laufschritt!*' We broke into a shambling trot, our calves nipped by guard dogs if we didn't move fast enough. With a superhuman effort we reached the camp entrance. As we left the railway track behind us we saw, snugly situated among the trees on either side, the SS barracks. Constructed in typically German military style, they looked well-maintained, even luxurious.

The gateway of the camp was surmounted by a bell-tower. Below it, in big Gothic letters, were the words '*RECHT ODER UNRECHT, MEIN VATERLAND*' (My country right or wrong).[1] I translated the inscription for those who had no German. At the gate we were counted and split up into groups of fifty. One batch crossed that fateful threshold every twenty minutes, once again at the double. At that rate it would be tomorrow before the entire trainload was processed. I couldn't help thinking of the men roasting inside their closed, unventilated boxcars.

---

[1] After the war, when Buchenwald was used as a detention camp for ex-Nazis, this motto was changed to '*JEDEM DAS SEINE*' (To each his own). It remains there to this day.

I myself formed part of the second batch and did not have too long to wait.

To the right of the buildings flanking the entrance was the tall brick chimney of the crematorium, a pleasant introduction to our new abode. We were doubled across a parade ground into a large, hangar-like building with a row of wooden tables along the rear wall. Here the Germans demonstrated their mysterious powers of organization, because I heard my name called. How did they know it, when I should by rights have been left behind in Paris? I could only conclude that Albrecht had added it to the list *en route*.

'Payraart!' The Germans' pronunciation always left much to be desired. It was my turn to step forward and answer another series of questions: name, date of birth, nationality, occupation, knowledge of foreign languages. The men who asked them were Kapos, or trusties in prison uniform. They should have been sympathetic to us, on the face of it, but their manner closely resembled that of the SS guards, which must have rubbed off on them. Instructed to hold out my arm,

287

I had it stamped in red with an 'F' and in black with the words 'POLITISCHER FRANZOSE' and a number which I now heard uttered for the first time: '77249 — *siebenundsiebzigzwoneunundvierzig!*' I was also instructed to surrender anything I possessed in the way of a wallet, ring or wristwatch. That was easy: everything had already been taken from me at Fresnes.

A long corridor with a counter on the right. Here we had to undress and relinquish our clothes, which were carefully stowed away in bags stamped with our numbers. I wasn't quick enough to suit the guard supervising us. Another trusty, identifiable by the green triangle on his sleeve, favoured me with a shower of blows from his truncheon. I wasn't the only one to undergo this treatment. The guard seemed to be rationing it out, because five prisoners would get through unscathed while the sixth received a drubbing.

Another long, low room with shower-heads set into the ceiling and airtight doors. Could it be one of the gas chambers of which we had heard such horrific rumours?

The doors remained open, the shower-heads gushed water. No gas for us — not yet, at all events. The water was cold but welcome. At the exit we had to immerse ourselves completely in a kind of sheep-dip filled with a strong solution of Lysol. It stung our cuts and sores and made our eyes smart so much we could hardly open them. Holding out our arms in front of us like blind men, we stumbled along under another hail of blows designed to habituate us to concentration camp discipline.

Next came a visit to the 'hairdresser'. Here we were made to kneel and shorn with clippers. Then, standing on a bench, we had the rest of our body hair removed. Another door said '*ARZT*', or doctor, but it didn't portend a medical inspection. All our bodily orifices were examined for hidden articles of value, so zealously that my anus was sore for several days.

Our next port of call was a big shed containing yet another counter with a sewing-machine at one end. Behind it were wooden shelves laden with masses of ragged clothing. Regardless of size, each of us was issued with the blue-and-white striped jacket and trousers of the concentration camp inmate, together with a pair of wooden clogs. We were also supposed to get caps, but there weren't enough to go round.

Holding up our over- or under-sized trousers with one hand because we had no string to serve as a belt, we shuffled along to the sewing-machine, where we had to exhibit the identification marks on our forearms and hand over our uniforms. Those who had already put them on were made to take them off — sufficient reason for another volley of blows and yells of '*Arschloch*! *Dummer Hund*!' Rectangles of white cloth bearing our number and a red triangle adorned with the letter 'F' were stitched to our jackets and trousers. Now that they had been marked in this way, it would be impossible to swap them with a taller or shorter fellow inmate.

I emerged from the shed with Marc Couturier, an acquaintance from Fresnes. We looked at each other and burst out laughing. With our shaven heads and ill-fitting garments, we might have been clowns taking part in some monstrous circus act. Our morale was good in spite of everything. We were happy to have left the confines of those stinking cattle wagons and the war would soon be over. We set off briskly down the broad avenue that led to the *Zeltlager*, or tented encampment.

On our left we could see the bulk of the wooden huts that housed the detainees. There were few to be seen, so we guessed they must be at work. Our own reception and transit camp was separated from the main camp by a high wire-mesh fence, so there was no way of communicating with any of the 'old boys'.

Although we had eaten nothing for three days, many of us urgently needed to relieve ourselves. I took an immediate dislike to the latrines, which required us to perch, parrot-like, on a tree trunk spanning a stinking ditch. Not yet inured to such sanitary facilities, we retched uncontrollably.

Our tents were pitched among the trees in a spot that might under other circumstances have seemed idyllic. They were eight-man tents, but thirty-six of us had to sleep on the bare ground inside. There was hardly room to move, and it was strictly forbidden to venture outside after evening roll-call. For the first time I saw watch-towers manned by armed SS guards and twin perimeter fences of electrified barbed wire.

There were still just over three thousand of us, but we learned that some of our number, among them the British prisoners, had been weeded out and confined in the Bunker, or camp jail. Not for the first time I had escaped by the skin of my teeth.

It rained all that night. We tried to drain off the water that flooded our tent by scooping out miniature ditches with our bare hands, but to little avail. The SS trooper who distributed our rations, a quarter of a loaf of bread apiece, deliberately tossed them into a puddle.

At ten the next morning the sun reappeared. It had only been a summer storm. Another downpour followed, but it didn't last long. Stark naked, we dried our clothes in the sun. I had kept track of the days: it was 24 August, 1944.

Fliegeralarm! The air-raid sirens wailed, the guards drove us back inside our tents. Lifting the canvas an inch or two, I saw a formation of bombers approaching. They were American 'Liberators'. Beneath them, strips of silver foil released to deceive the Germans' radar-operated anti-aircraft guns drifted down like a huge shoal of whitebait.

All at once came the unmistakable whistle of falling bombs, then a series of explosions and the hot breath of the resulting blast. The SS guards could be heard shouting orders. Was the camp itself under attack — possibly, even, about to be liberated by Allied paratroops? Some of the prisoners started singing, only to be silenced by a burst of machine-gun fire from one of the watch-towers.

It was, in fact, the Gustlof factory adjoining the camp that had been bombed. Dark clouds of smoke were rising into the air and mingling with the fumes from the crematorium chimney. Several thousand inmates worked in the factory and many had been delivered from their sufferings for ever. Prisoners, being less than human, were not entitled to take cover during air raids.

SS men were posted all round the perimeter fence, which was electrified no longer. The bombs had not only cut off the power but blown gaps in the wire and there were fears of a mass escape. Prisoners belonging to outside working parties were marched back into camp. Bursts of machine-gun fire told us that our guards were on the warpath. We kept our heads down.

The next day a company of Wehrmacht soldiers entered our enclosure. The SS men were busy licking their wounds elsewhere.

'Get ready to move out!' The soldiers didn't even count us before doubling us back the way we had come and out through the sinister gateway. Noticing as we passed the SS barracks that some of them had been destroyed, we breathed a thank-you to the airmen who had risked flying low enough to bomb them with precision while leaving the prisoners' quarters untouched. We felt heartened, having been subjected to no ill-treatment by the ordinary soldiers who escorted us from the Zeltlager to the waiting train, which consisted of open goods wagons.

We were soon disillusioned by the sight of SS troopers lining the track with their dogs. The wagons had been used for transporting coal and were thick with black dust. Hauled aboard by those who had already clambered into them, we settled down to wait.

One man's leg, which was dangling over the edge of the wagon, got crushed when its hinged side was raised and slammed shut. Released in response to his screams of pain, he tumbled to the ground and lay there writhing. A guard walked up, turned him over with his boot, and put him out of his misery with two bullets in the head.

Another SS man climbed on to the brakesman's platform and covered us with his sub-machine gun. The train got under way. Our relief at bidding farewell to Buchenwald was mingled with foreboding. Our destination might be even less desirable.

15

Dora

NORDHAUSEN was, and still is, a small town situated among the foothills of the Harz Mountains, on the edge of the North German plain. About ten kilometres from there, dominated by the Kohnstein, was the so-called 'K. L. Mittelbau Dora', a labour camp so secret that it rated a '*Nacht and Nebel*' ('night and fog', or top secret) classification, meaning that the only way an inmate could be permitted to leave there was by way of the crematorium chimney.

The journey from Buchenwald had taken only a few hours. Some 2500 of us were left by the time we entered the gates of our new 'holiday camp', which were surmounted by the motto '*ARBEIT MACHT FREI*' (loosely, 'Work to Gain Your Freedom').

The column of prisoners trudged slowly

towards the camp along railway tracks that led to two huge caverns hewn out of the mountainside. On our right SS men could be seen emerging from the huts that served as their living quarters; on our left was a marshalling yard with some big, hollow metal cylinders arrayed on it. Were they aircraft fuselages, I wondered, or could they be casings for the flying bombs of which we had heard rumours? A row of flatcars had been shunted into some sidings. They were carefully shrouded in tarpaulins, but the shapes beneath them gave the game away: this was indeed a factory for the production of the V2, the *second* of the '*Vergeltungswaffen*', or retaliatory weapons, with which Hitler hoped to bring the British to their knees.

Some prisoners emerged from one of the tunnels pushing a wagon, among them a Frenchman identified as such by the 'F' on his jacket. We asked him where we were. He signed to us not to speak, but we heard him mutter a single word: 'Dora.'

A shiver ran down my spine. Some long-term prisoners at Buchenwald had told us through the wire what the name signified: the labour camp from which no one ever returned. Dora was a Moloch that had consumed over twenty thousand prisoners in a single year. *ARBEIT MACHT FREI* . . . Perhaps, but the freedom in question was release from this earthly life.

Now that we were safely inside the camp our SS guards left us, their job done, and turned us over to the 'Greens' and 'Blacks' who replaced them with an efficiency worthy of their masters. Wielding their truncheons with a will, the Kapos drove us across the parade ground to the gallows on the far side.

'Form up, stand at attention, caps off!' We had no caps, but it seemed that this order was a traditional prelude to the ritual that followed. The SS Rapportführer, or second-in-command of the camp, made his appearance escorted by a 'Green', the Lagerältester (senior trusty), and the Lagerdolmetscher (camp interpreter).

Most of us were French. A long roll-call ensued. Then the Rapportführer addressed us. 'You're filthy swine, the lot of you,' he began. 'You must keep yourselves clean, learn to wash.'

It was true that our outward appearance hadn't been improved by our sojourn in the mud at Buchenwald. The SS had an obsessive fear of lice. *EINE LAUS DEIN TODT*! (One Louse Can Spell Your Death!) was posted up all over the camp.

'You're here to work,' the Rapportführer went on. There followed a litany devoted to the glory of the Third Reich and the way in which, by manufacturing weapons that would annihilate the barbarian hordes and the degenerate politicians who had betrayed us, we would be helping to create an earthly paradise destined to endure for a thousand years. 'That is what our Führer, Adolf Hitler, has promised us. While waiting for the day of final victory to dawn, let us give unstintingly of our sweat and blood!'

It was a thoroughly Wagnerian performance. The man's unawareness of his country's imminent and inexorable defeat was puerile. After all, he was addressing Frenchmen who already knew that Paris had been liberated. He was mad, but that didn't make him any less dangerous from the point of view of prisoners who, like us, were at the mercy of his delusions.

The blocks near the entrance to the camp were embellished with flower-beds and the walkways had been asphalted. Was it possible that Dora had changed? The descriptions we'd been given were very different. We soon discovered this was only window-dressing, scenery on a stage where horrific real-life dramas were enacted daily.

'No work today. Tomorrow you'll be assigned your duties.'

We were deloused once more, then marched off to our respective huts, which had to be cleaned from top to bottom. At last we were dismissed to our Lysol-impregnated palliasses. It was the first night we had slept under a roof since Fresnes, albeit four to a bunk.

Four a.m. '*Fertigmachen!*' We tumbled out of our bunks, those who lingered being assisted to the floor with blows from a truncheon. For once the roll was called outside the block. A 'Green' sang out our numbers in German, which few of the Frenchmen understood. More chaos ensued as we were divided into four working parties, each under the command of a Kapo overseer and one or more 'Green' Vorarbeiter (foremen) who took it in turns to shower us with blows and abuse. Then, finding it hard to keep our wooden-soled clogs on our feet, we were doubled off to join some other working parties drawn up on the central parade-ground.

Columns of prisoners were already emerging from the tunnels, their faces grey and drawn with fatigue. They were the night shift that would be taking over our bunks. Visible in the harsh glare of floodlights, the camp clock now said 5 a.m. Just inside the entrance, where we had been counted on arrival, a dozen-odd gypsy fiddlers were playing a species of military march. Wreathed in morning mist, they presented a weird picture reminiscent of the witches' sabbath dances that feature in the legends of the Harz Mountains.

The night shift marched off with guard-dogs snapping at their heels. At the entrances to the tunnels our group, comprising some three hundred men, was split up into two working parties. One entered the cavernous main tunnel while the other was detailed to carry rails along the secondary shaft. The gauge was universal, so why not load them on to flatcars and push them straight in? Was this another mysterious aspect of German 'organization'? The mystery was solved when I finally entered the subterranean hell that awaited us: the flatcars were reserved for the engines of death being manufactured there.

Teams: six men to a rail. Distance to be covered: nearly two kilometres from the outside world to the point where zombies encrusted with white dust were attacking the rock and enlarging the underground chambers and galleries. We were soon exhausted, but any sign of flagging brought a hail of blows. A Frenchman ahead of me, in an instinctively self-defensive gesture, grabbed the stick that was being used to belabour him. He was shot down in cold blood by an SS guard, presumably *pour encourager les autres*.

Once, in those unimaginably far-off days before the war, I had seen a film purporting to show how the ancient Egyptians had employed slaves to build the Pyramids. Compared to the nightmare vision that now met my eyes, it was a sentimental idyll. Deep in the black bowels of the earth, living skeletons with dead eyes, their backs bowed beneath incessant blows, toiled away in the blinding glare of floodlights. Confronted by the spectacle of the men at the rock face, we considered ourselves lucky to be carrying rails.

The secondary shaft, which ran parallel to the main tunnel, was barely wide enough to accommodate us rail-carriers and the tip-wagons laden with spoil. We were in danger of being crushed every time they passed.

I spent three weeks with this detail, some of whose members found it more lethal working outside in the rain and mud than toting rails along the tunnel. On two occasions several of us were summoned to carry out cleaning work in the main tunnel and lateral chambers.

This was where the V2s, the rockets intended to devastate England, were manufactured under the supervision of

German engineers who had to be addressed as '*Meister*'. Omnipresent SD men were posted there to enforce discipline and good order, because cases of sabotage were frequent. The subterranean complex formed an assembly line: the nearer the monstrous rockets got to the mouth of the tunnel, the nearer completion they were. It was an impressive spectacle — one that might have sprung from the imagination of Jules Verne and showed that his flights of fancy were far from wide of the mark. The rocket engines, electronic components and guidance mechanisms were manufactured in the lateral chambers, the assembly work took place in the main tunnel. In blatant contravention of the rules of war, which Nazism trampled underfoot, these tasks were performed by prisoners. All too many such courageous men were suspected of sabotage or caught in the act and executed.

★ ★ ★

Autumn was far advanced and the flowers in the bed outside our block had withered. We were greeted one night on returning from work by the news that we were to be transferred next morning, presumably to Ellrich, a camp on the other side of the mountain, where more tunnels were being excavated. The deathrate there was so high that, like Dora in its early days, the ogre needed constant feeding with replacements.

Some two thousand of us lined up outside the administrative blocks, five hundred less than had left Buchenwald. They had already gone up in smoke — literally.

The loudspeakers crackled into life. '77249 fall out!' That was me! Why, what had I done? What new ordeal lay in store for me?

The main body of prisoners marched past Block 28, the Kapos' brothel, and disappeared through the gates. In all, eight of us had been told to fall out. We were collected by a man from the 'labour statistics' department, a German political prisoner named Lucius, who conducted us to another block. It seemed that we had been transferred to the Lagerkommando, the detail employed at camp headquarters.

I was issued with a new pair of trousers — the first had succumbed to guard-dogs' teeth — and told to report to the infirmary to have my oozing cuts dressed. There I was tended by a young French doctor named Paul Pébeyre, a prisoner like myself. For want of anything better, he sewed up my cuts with an ordinary needle and thread. There was a danger of infection, but saliva is excellent for promoting scar tissue. From now on, in order to lick the cuts in question, I had to go through a daily routine worthy of a contortionist.

I did no work that first day. After roll-call in my new block I was summoned to the office of the Blockältester, or senior trusty, a 'Red' German, and invited to sit down. 'You've nothing to fear,' he said affably, 'we're all friends here.' Another two prisoners came in, both Frenchmen. They were Pierre Dejussieu and Émile Bollaert, with whom I'd had dealings shortly after my arrival in Paris the year before. Pierre, known as 'Poncaral' in the Resistance, had been arrested late in 1943, but it was news to me that Bollaert had suffered the same fate and that both men had wound up at Dora.

It was Pierre, the only other person aware that I was a parachute agent, who had spotted me in the tunnel and alerted the internal resistance network. Professor Dr Sonnenfeld, a courageous German political prisoner, had been instrumental in retrieving me from the ranks of those who were almost certainly doomed to die. My lucky star had protected me yet again.

Speaking in low voices, because walls had ears and informers were rife in camp, my new-found friends put me in the picture. I had already guessed that, whatever they expected of me, my task would be a difficult and dangerous one. I was to remain with the Lagerkommando until a position of importance to the organization fell vacant. Meantime I would be employed by the *Schreibstube* as an 'errand boy'. To enable me to do this, I was given a pass that allowed me relative freedom of movement all over the camp. My new status gave me invaluable 'cover' for my other new rôle as a form of liaison officer for the Resistance Group. I felt happy and hopeful at the prospect of once more making myself useful on behalf of the cause we all served.

Confucius wrote: 'The height of misfortune is the loss of all hope.' I now had an aim to pursue and a reason to go on living. To die in this place would be stupid, I felt, and I resolved to deny my tormentors the satisfaction.

By virtue of my rôle as a contact man I got to know most of the members of the network. More numerous than I would have guessed, they were secreted in the ranks of every working party. One of them, Pierre Rozan, had even been assigned to the camp commandant, Obersturmbannführer (SS Lieutenant-Colonel) Hans Moser, as his batman and general factotum. The others included Pierre Ziller, Bernard Zuber, Bordier, Chandon, Unterreiner, Dr Poupault and Lenoir, a postmaster who had occupied a cell above mine at Fresnes and with whom I used to converse via the latrine pipe. Like so many more whose names escape my memory, they were men of honour with a single aim in view: to serve a just cause and contribute to the survival of their comrades.

308

I also got to know the German 'Greens', so called because of the green triangles on their prison uniforms. They needed handling with special care. Convicted criminals who co-operated with the camp authorities in return for a promise that their sentences would be commuted when the war was won, they were malevolent sadists ready to do anything for their Nazi masters. The most dangerous of them, beyond a doubt, were Blockältester George Willax and Kapos Willy Zwicher and Karl Kohla, the latter being in charge of executions.

December came, enveloping the camp in a white shroud of snow and ice. The evening roll-calls were interminable. Lying in a heap beside those who could still stand were the corpses of those who had failed to survive the last few hours. The numbers never tallied because one or two prisoners had crawled beneath their huts to die like sick animals. They had to be found, which meant that a roll-call could take as long as four hours. Meanwhile, other men collapsed and fell, frozen to death in their tracks.

The news that reached us via clandestine

radios was disheartening. The Germans had launched a major offensive in the Ardennes and were driving the Allies back. The SS guards' spirits revived. They indulged in an orgy of brutality and the 'Greens' followed suit. Flatcars laden with naked corpses, each man's chest inscribed with his number in blue indelible ink, rolled up daily from Ellrich and other outside camps. The so-called crematorium squad was kept busy day and night. Evil-smelling smoke pervaded every corner of the camp and clung to our clothes. Woe betide any prisoners from camp headquarters who ventured too close to the crematorium. '*Du und du, mithelfen!*' came the bellowed order, and they would have to help unload the bodies. One day I myself was called upon to perform this special chore. It required a thick skin and a strong stomach.

Two of us climbed on to the flatcar. Grabbing an arm and a leg apiece, we swung the corpses over the side. Below us, another prisoner noted down the numbers while the SS man beside him prised open the dead men's jaws and a member of the Sonderkommando (special squad) stood ready to extract any gold teeth with a pair of pliers. Among the bodies I spotted a former classmate of mine, Dady Marq, son of a law professor at the Université Libre in Brussels. The concealment of all emotion was essential to one's own survival, but I have always been haunted by the memory of Dady's upturned eyes and gaping mouth, which seemed to be uttering a final plea for help.

One of the disadvantages of assignment to the Lagerkommando was that it exposed one to the risk of being summoned to the infirmary for use as a guinea-pig by the SS doctors who conducted experiments there. This happened to me early on, because Dr Cespiva, Obersturmführer Dr Kahr's assistant, had seen me having my dog bites treated. One of my lacerated legs was deliberately contaminated with excrement, the other anointed with some evil-smelling brown ointment. The latter healed swiftly, the former turned blue, and I began to experience shooting pains in the groin. Cespiva examined me daily, noting the spread of infection in one leg and the healing process in the other. After several days he pronounced me 'ripe for treatment', and I was given a week's course of injections in the left-hand side of my chest. Miraculously, the incipient gangrene was cured. My only memento is an assortment of scars on my left leg and an understandable dread of hypodermic needles. This experiment, which was certainly conclusive, may have benefited some German soldiers wounded in action.

Just before Christmas my Blockältester informed me that I had been transferred from the Lagerkommando to the *Häftlingsbekleidungskammer* (prisoners' clothing store). This constituted 'promotion', in that it numbered me among the camp's most favoured inmates, but the task that devolved on me was a dangerous one. It would be up to me not to get caught.

The 'Kammer', as it was called for short, was a large building standing apart from the accommodation blocks. It contained four well-appointed offices, one of them having a small inner sanctum furnished with armchairs. This was the domain of the Oberscharführer

(SS quartermaster-sergeant) in charge of the premises. The second office was occupied, between their tours of inspection, by a couple of Romanian SS men, and the remaining two were assigned to us. They housed a card index listing all the civilian clothes and personal possessions — wallets, watches, rings, etc — which had been taken from prisoners and forwarded from the places where they had been arrested.

This meticulous storing and cataloguing of personal effects — articles that would not pass to the German state until their owners were dead — was typical of the inordinate bureaucracy prevailing in Nazi Germany. It also contrasted starkly with the minimal value attached to a prisoner's life.

Neatly suspended from hooks in the main bay were the numbered bags that contained prisoners' clothes, shoes included. A smaller annexe was devoted to rows of filing cabinets filled with envelopes, also numbered, containing articles of value. Curiosity made me look for the envelope bearing my own number, 77249. Sure enough, there were the watch, ring, fountain pen and wallet (minus papers) that had been taken from me at Fresnes.

The task assigned me by the Resistance committee was a tricky one. I was to purloin woollen and other warm underclothes for the benefit of fellow prisoners whose work exposed them to the cold, thereby helping them to survive. At the end of the day these had to be secreted beneath my own clothes and handed over to another member of the organization, a half-German, half-French Saarländer named Schreiner, who slept in my block and was in charge of distribution. Although this change of employment meant that I no longer had any official reason to be moving round the camp, I had managed to keep my invaluable little 'chit', with its eagle-on-swastika stamp and this was a great help in my resistance role.

The Kammer's existing personnel included three other prisoners whom Émile Bollaert described as 'all right'. I was to persuade them to assist me in my task, but without completely involving them in it. They were not, for instance, to know anything about the other members of the network. The three men in question were Janko Pobureny, a Polish schoolteacher, Jan Petra, a Czech chemical engineer from Prague, and Paul Capelle, a captain in the Belgian air force.

Our duties consisted in keeping the card index, removing dead prisoners' effects, hanging up the clothes bags of new arrivals, and filing their effects. The last job was becoming rarer, however, because the German administrative machine was starting to seize up. Personal effects had ceased to be forwarded as promptly, and most of those we received came from other camps evacuated in the path of the Russian advance.

Particulars were transmitted to us by the Schreibstube, or camp orderly room. We were thus in possession of the names, numbers and dates of birth or death of the entire work force of Dora and neighbouring camps. A prisoner's official and actual date of death differed by several days, the former being the date on which his body arrived at Dora for cremation. Missing from the list were those who had died in outside camps and been summarily buried in mass graves.

I hit on the idea of creating a second card index and mentioned the matter to Pierre Dejussieu, who approved. If it could be hidden and preserved from destruction before the camp was liberated, it would form a valuable record and an aid to tracing those who had disappeared. All that remained was to obtain the approval of our SS boss. Keen to prove himself an efficient administrator of state 'assets', he agreed.

I never knew the Scharführer's surname, but his SS comrades called him 'Uli'. He was a portly, jovial sexagenarian with a taste for little luxuries. His office was never without a vase of flowers, and the handsome carpet and old prints had probably been 'organized' when he was stationed in Holland. A music-lover, he possessed a gramophone and a number of classical records, even including some Mendelssohn, a composer banned by Hitler on racial grounds. A bottle of his favourite wine, a fruity Spätlese, always stood ready to hand on a small side table. Uli had been an accountant in civilian life. He was married with three children of whom two had been killed on the Eastern Front. His desk was adorned with their photographs in full-dress uniform, as well as pictures of his wife and surviving child, a daughter. A native of Magdeburg, he had lost his home in an Allied air raid.

Uli was a perfectionist with a love of order and cleanliness. Such was his aversion to concentration camp uniform that, on arriving for work in the morning, we had to raid the bags hanging in the main store-room and change into civilian clothes. That was how I came to retrieve my own, which were still in tolerably good condition. The same ritual was performed in the evening, but in reverse. Another of his aversions was the sight of our shaven heads, so he issued us with *Haarscheine* (hair permits), duly signed by the camp commandant, which authorized us to grow crew-cuts in the Wehrmacht manner.

Janko, Jan and I spoke German together, and Uli, quickly gathering that we were his intellectual superiors, developed a certain respect for us. His benevolence did not extend to Paul, who, being an airman, was one of the breed who had destroyed his home.

Because he did not find his work engrossing, Uli often invited us to keep him company, one by one, and listen to music or chat with him. He was a lonely man, shattered and disoriented by the war that had robbed him of his sons, and his faith in Hitler had perceptibly waned. And yet . . .

My father, having observed the rise of National Socialism during the 1930s, had warned me in his capacity as a psychiatrist of the ambivalence latent in the German psyche. I soon got a demonstration of this.

One day, after listening to Beethoven's Pastoral Symphony, Uli offered us a reward for our excellent administrative work on his behalf: permission to accompany him to '*eine schöne Sonderer-hängung*' (a nice, special hanging) to be carried out behind the Bunker. He never fathomed our reasons for politely declining his invitation. 'But he's only a criminal,' he protested, 'a German communist traitor.'

Germans condemned to death by the Gestapo did not suffer the same fate as those of other nationalities. Not for them a collective execution at Sunday roll-call in the presence of their fellow prisoners. A German, even one convicted of high treason, could not be allowed to expire under the gaze of his racial inferiors.

The cynicism of our kindly, accommodating SS boss, with his pretensions to culture, made my blood run cold. Although he was so 'broadminded' that we sometimes ventured to discuss politics with him, I had no doubt that, when or if the occasion arose, he would blithely send us to the gallows without the least compunction.

The execution of non-Germans condemned to death in camp was a theatrical performance of a different kind. Once a week, preferably on Sunday, all prisoners except those at work in the tunnels had to form up in front of the gallows on the edge of the parade-ground. The condemned men, with their wrists pinioned behind them and wooden gags between their teeth, were led out and lined up in sixes beneath the long beam with the nooses dangling from it.

'*Achtung*!' Oberscharführer Sander of the SD would read out the sentence: '*Tod durch den Strang*' (death by hanging). It was only while those words were being pronounced that everyone had to stand at attention. The hanging itself, being the liquidation of an expendable prisoner, was unimportant and did not merit such an honour.

The nooses were placed around the men's necks and the executioner turned the handle that winched up the beam, slowly throttling the unfortunates to death. Once they had stopped kicking and been taken down, an SS man put a bullet in the back of each neck. That done, the corpses were transported to the crematorium.

Communication No. SIV D2-450/42g-81 of 6 January, 1942, signed by Heinrich Himmler, Reichsführer-SS and Chief of the German Police, was quite specific:

'Hanging is to be carried out by detainees; wherever possible, in the case of foreign workers, by members of the same ethnic group. Detainees will each receive three cigarettes per execution.'

No SS man ever hanged a prisoner; therefore he merely gave the order to do so.

★ ★ ★

Tomorrow would be Christmas Eve. For some days now, a handful of us had been paying surreptitious nocturnal visits to the blocks in the upper reaches of the camp which housed most of the French, Belgian and Dutch prisoners employed inside the tunnel. They were badly in need of moral support. It would soon be 1945 — 'liberation year', we felt sure — but it was essential that comrades more deprived than ourselves should preserve their determination to survive. With the approval of three 'Blockälteste', we organized a Christmas party for them.

Some days earlier a Norwegian prisoner had told me about a legend current in his native land. It seemed that in prehistoric times, even before the Viking era, when the days were at their shortest and the sun was just a fleeting glow on the horizon, men used to emerge from their caves, build an enormous bonfire and celebrate around it. Friends and enemies shook hands and planted a young fir tree in the soil thawed out by the heat of the fire. That fir tree, with its evergreen foliage, symbolized life, hope and the miracle of renewal.

And the miracle took place. At roll-call on Christmas Eve a big bonfire was set ablaze on the parade-ground not far from the gallows, and a fir tree, illuminated by a spotlight, stood silhouetted against the flames. We eyed it warily, half suspecting some diabolical trick designed to plunge us still deeper into despair.

But nothing untoward occurred. Our Norwegian comrade's legend went the rounds. Skeletal, bent-backed figures raised their heads and supported those for whom this Christmas Eve might well be their last night on earth. The gypsy fiddlers massacred *Silent Night*. Roll-call was shorter than usual. We weren't even counted, the Germans being in too much of a hurry to celebrate Christmas and their successes in the Ardennes. Dismissed, we headed for our respective blocks.

The news spread like wildfire: No work in the tunnel tonight! All prisoners free to associate! Only a few guards patrolled the camp.

As the price of his silence, the Blockältester of Block 137 had been presented with a bottle of schnapps purloined by one of us from the SS barracks. The same source furnished cigarettes and even chocolate taken from parcels addressed to prisoners but never distributed by our masters, who reserved them for their own delectation. I turned up at the party bearing two warm vests and, for one of my friends, a snapshot of his wife and children filched from his envelope in the Kammer files.

The Norwegian legend was told and retold, and we shook hands all round, heartened by the belief that we might yet survive against all the odds. The brothers Jean-Louis and Pierre Gaillot, both of them dentists employed in the camp infirmary, had composed some songs in which we all joined. Then, quite suddenly, a powerful baritone voice rang out from the shadows at the back of the hut. Nothing could have seemed more moving or appropriate than the exiles' chorus from Verdi's *Nabucco*.

It was late when the *Marseillaise* brought our all too brief spell of relaxation to an end, but by then the pall of gloom enshrouding the prison camp had been rent asunder. We returned to our own blocks comforted and refreshed.

'On earth peace, goodwill toward men . . .'

We heard next day that, after our return, a drama had unfolded in the Russian accommodation blocks. Encouraged by the peaceful atmosphere and the absence of guards, the Russians had planned a mass escape during the night. Unluckily for them, their scheme was betrayed by an Italian Blockältester named Grosso, who overheard them discussing it in their sleeping quarters. Twenty-four of them were hanged soon afterwards.

One of our SS guards owned a dog that had the run of the camp, a plump, well-fed dachshund of friendly, playful disposition. One day we had an amusing idea: What if we ate it? Our amusing idea became an obsession, and various proposals were advanced for putting it into effect. It was Paul Capelle who came up with an absolute brainwave: electrocution!

The problem was how to avoid getting caught. Although failure would mean the gallows, Paul's scheme was ingenious enough to have tempted Old Nick himself. There were three of us in the team. We had discovered a place behind the Kammer, only twelve or fifteen metres from the wire, where we couldn't be seen from the nearest watch-tower. It was the ideal spot. 'Egon', as we'd heard his master call him, had a fondness for chasing after sticks and that sealed his fate. Paul undertook to throw a stick at the electrified wire while I kept watch from a distance. Then it would be my turn to go into action. Everything went according to plan: a shower of sparks and the dachshund lay dead in the gap between the two fences.

I went to the guard-room at the gate. The sentry gave me the ritual order to remove my cap — '*Mütze ab!*' — and asked what I wanted. 'There's a dog lying dead inside the fence,' I replied. 'I know,' he said, 'it belongs to that fool Karl. He's away on leave.' I stood my ground. 'What's to be done?' I asked. The sentry's answer fulfilled all my hopes. 'You'd better yank it out, I suppose. I'll send someone with you.'

My SS escort was a Romanian who had little love for the Germans. Armed with the long, insulated rake customarily used for dislodging dead leaves from the foot of the fence, I recovered Egon's carcass. The Romanian relieved me of the rake. 'You throw dog away,' he told me in his fractured German, and walked off.

Several Russians who had witnessed the operation were only waiting for a chance to rob me of my prey, but Paul and Jan had remained on the alert and came to my rescue just in time. Egon was butchered in our hut that night and made an excellent meal.

Prisoners continued to arrive by the trainload, day after day. They weren't 'new boys'. Living corpses transferred to

Dora from camps in the east such as Gross-Rosen, Treblinka, Auschwitz, and even Mauthausen, they were in transit and would, if they survived for long enough, be forwarded to nearby camps such as Ellrich and Harzungen. Many of them died before this could happen. The crematorium was now working flat out and it was rumoured that mass graves had been dug in the woods to accommodate the overflow.

The new arrivals included a contingent of Italian soldiers who had deserted to the partisans. Too disorganized to be effective, they had been overwhelmed by superior German forces, taken prisoner and consigned to a concentration camp. Many of these men, who were officially designated terrorists, still wore the uniform of Mussolini's fascist army.

Dora now held nearly 30,000 inmates. Our daily ration, which in 'better' days had consisted of 200 grams of bread, 15 grams of margarine and a litre of watery turnip soup, sometimes with a small slice of sausage or an anonymous morsel of meat afloat in it, had now shrunk to a few mouthfuls of noisome liquid and a hunk of what passed for bread.

Despite the news of Allied successes in the west, friction made itself felt among the prisoners. Carried away by Soviet successes in the east and resentful of our lack of support before the war, the Poles and Czechs became uppish and formed themselves in gangs. The Ukrainians, knowing that their country had now been liberated, joined in with a will. At night, armed with cudgels, they looted the huts that housed 'westerners'.

Our guards looked on idly and made no attempt to prevent these forays, which often ended in murder. That foreign inmates should kill each other was a fact of no importance, but woe betide anyone who molested a 'Green'. That spelled the gallows, as the marauders well knew, so they didn't risk it. Indeed, they even enjoyed the protection of certain Kapos and other bloodthirsty overseers.

We no longer ventured out of our huts at night. This posed a new problem for the resistance network and disrupted our system of communication.

It was rumoured that Albrecht Speer,

Hitler's Minister of War Production, was going to establish his headquarters in the subterranean factory. New buildings sprang up on the slope below the SS barracks. Work went on day and night, so the project was clearly considered urgent.

The growing influx of prisoners presented another problem: the camp's stock of uniforms ran out. We had to withdraw batches of civilian clothes from the Kammer and take them to the so-called tailoring department, where scissors and sewing-machines were in constant use. Pieces of cloth were removed from the sides of the trousers and the backs and sleeves of the jackets and replaced with patches of blue-and-white striped material cut from scarce, cannibalized uniforms. The first to be issued with these heterogeneous garments, which were hardly worthy of Balenciaga or Cardin, were the tunnel workers. The Lagerkommando and the Kammer detail got them later.

I had always been firmly convinced, ever since my arrest, that if there was even a fifty-fifty chance of escape I ought to take it. Careful preparation was essential, however, and civilian clothes were an indispensable prerequisite of success.

In the course of my daily perambulations among the Kammer's rows of clothing bags I had unearthed a British battledress top, some trousers that had belonged to a French soldier of my own build, a pair of brown boots and a khaki shirt and socks. On the pretext that my wooden-soled clogs were worn out, I obtained Uli's permission to wear the socks and boots. The other garments made their way to my block one by one.

Janko the Pole, who had a friend in the tailoring department, got him to sew on my blue-and-white patches without removing the material beneath. To prevent anyone from detecting this subterfuge, he neatly sewed equivalent patches on the inside as well. At my request he also gave me a triangle of green cloth and a needle and thread.

Thus equipped, I could, once I got away, pass myself off as one of the many prisoners of war who worked in semi-freedom on German farms. I was ready to go. I had become the organization's expert on procuring underclothes for comrades who lacked them. One day, however, my luck almost deserted me.

Our two guards at the Kammer were Romanians, as I have already said. Wounded on the Eastern Front while fighting alongside the Germans, they had been classified unfit for combat duty and assigned to the camps. Some members of the Romanian SS were 'all right' but others exceptionally cruel.

I was concealing a sweater under my own clothes when I suddenly froze: Absalon, one of our two Romanians, was watching me. My goose was cooked, I thought, but no, he made a disapproving gesture and continued his tour of inspection. Our paths crossed again a little later. '*Das könnte gefährlich sein, auch für mich*' (That could be dangerous for me as well), he said. He had not only seen but understood everything.

A year later, when my search for war criminals took me to a Belgian internment camp near Waterloo, I caught sight of Absalon in a group of SS prisoners. I submitted a detailed report on his good behaviour in the camp, including his failure to denounce me, and he was released soon afterwards.

As the days went by certain departments of the Ministry of War Production moved into the tunnel. It seemed clear to us that Speer was anxious to save his own skin. The SS guards mysteriously disappeared, reportedly to Nordhausen, and were replaced by older Wehrmacht personnel. The Allies had established a bridgehead at Remagen, on the German side of the Rhine, and were now advancing rapidly.

Ministry personnel and the managers of the underground factory had no wish to be classified as war criminals, even though they had witnessed or actively promoted the atrocities perpetrated there. Even the 'Greens' had changed their tune. As for Uli, he had disappeared from the Kammer with the other SS men. Since he was the only outsider aware of the existence of our second card index, we concealed it in the roof space.

Miraculously, there was a distribution of prisoners' parcels — or, rather, of as much of them as our guards had left behind in the SS barracks. The food was putrid, but some inmates were so hungry that they risked eating it and died of botulism.

A battle of wills was in progress between Himmler and Speer. The former wanted to exterminate Dora's work force before the camp was overrun because of its top secret 'Nacht und Nebel' classification, but Speer firmly opposed this. As a compromise, the men of the Wehrmacht and Volksturm (territorial home guard) who now guarded the camp were provisionally enrolled by SS officers. Hauptscharführer (sergeant-major) Hans Busta, the torturer of Dachau, was appointed second-in-command to Moser, the camp commandant, whom the Gestapo considered too 'soft'. We were still in mortal danger.

One afternoon wave after wave of American bombers dropped incendiaries on Nordhausen, eleven kilometres away. The sky glowed red all night long as flames leapt into the air above the devastated town.

Next morning the new boss of the clothing store, a man in his late sixties, treated us to a brief speech. 'This is the end. Hitler and his henchmen are insane — they've done for us!' Head bowed in dejection, he retired to his office. Through the glass panel we saw him sit down and produce a bottle of schnapps from his briefcase. He also took out some photographs and laid them on the desk, then started to write, weeping as he did so. We watched him without compassion, telling ourselves that it was his turn to suffer now.

A minute or two later, while we were going about our business, a shot rang out. We hurried into the office accompanied by two dismayed guards. The man had committed suicide. His head was resting on the letter he'd just written. It was addressed to his granddaughter, the only surviving member of his family. Here, as nearly as I can recall, is what it said:

Karin,
Your grandfather was never a Nazi, but years ago he was weak and foolish enough to believe what the Nazis said. The iniquities of the régime dawned on me as time went by, notably when

a great friend of mine was taken away by the Gestapo, never to be seen again. He was a Jew. He was also a good German. I now know what happened to him. This crazy war has taught me that much.

I am guilty. Had I opposed the régime in its infancy, others might have followed my lead. I was a coward dazzled by a New Order that promised us a thousand years of happiness and prosperity. Life will not be easy for you. May you have what I lacked, the courage of your convictions and respect for the individual, even if, at school, you have been taught otherwise.

I send you my love. Now I must pay the price.

His poignant admission and posthumous advice put me in mind of something my father had told me a long time before, when Nazism first reared its head: 'Taken as individuals, the Germans are a race of weaklings.'

It was ten o'clock when we heard the sound of aircraft approaching — not heavy bombers, they were flying too

335

fast and low. Several formations of Thunderbolts machine-gunned the tunnel entrances and dropped bombs on the military sector of the camp. Being situated at its highest point, we had a perfect view of the raid in progress. Chaos reigned, figures running in all directions. Smoke began to issue from the mouth of the main tunnel. Prisoners on the day shift emerged from the secondary shaft and were redirected to the entrance to our camp. Others were assigned to fight the fires.

Going in search of news, I met Pierre Rozan coming in the opposite direction. He told me that all work had ceased. It seemed that the fire in the tunnel had not been caused by the air raid. Some said it was sabotage, because the SD had launched an investigation. The blaze had started in the engineers' offices, which were almost deserted. Most of the engineers were billeted in Nordhausen, so they were either burying their dead or salvaging what remained of their possessions from the ruins of the town.

Lucius and several other 'politicals' had vanished from our block. Knowing that the SD were after them, they had made themselves scarce and taken refuge with their Russian friends in the blocks at the top of the camp. They had, in fact, declared war on their 'Green' compatriots, who had gone to ground in a block of their own. Lucius tried to foment a general uprising, but the Polish and Russian group were too wary to join in.

The SS had come back to re-establish their own brand of order. Work in the tunnel was at a standstill and anarchy reigned, but our 'western' group wasn't strong or well-organized enough to go into action. The 'Greens', of whom too many had survived, were on the war path assisted by SS troopers.

Every block was systematically searched and woe betide anyone who drew attention to himself while the search was in progress. Then we were ordered to assemble on the parade-ground — all of us without exception: even the moribund inmates of the infirmary had to turn out.

Darkness fell, turning the scene into a Walpurgis Night phantasmagoria. Only the legendary witches of the Harz Mountains were missing from roll-call, but they seemed to be hovering all around us in the harsh glare of the floodlights. The gypsy orchestra continued to scrape away throughout the ten long hours we were compelled to remain standing on that chill March night.

A few prisoners had been segregated near the gallows. Their ranks were steadily swelled by other unfortunates whose hiding places had been discovered. Before long there were nearly 200 of them, picked out by spotlights and ringed by SS men and dogs as they were made to kneel there with their hands on their heads.

Additional, larger gallows had been erected. In groups of twenty, the men were hoisted off the ground by their necks and left to kick until death supervened. Lucius was one of those who breathed his last that night.

This reign of terror continued unabated for forty-eight hours. The crematorium was in constant use, the SD's 'political section' busily combed the files for other prisoners who deserved to hang. One by one doomed men were dragged from their huts and marched off to the gallows, which never stood idle. Luckily for me, my file had been removed and destroyed by a fellow detainee. He was already dead, I was still alive.

Then the purge came to an end and our SS guards were once more replaced by army personnel. Although no work was done, the camp resumed an air of normality. Trains consisting of cattle wagons were being assembled in the sidings beyond the gates. We guessed that we would soon be on the move again.

I learned from one of the soldiers that Himmler had given orders for us to be walled up in the tunnel, there to die of hunger and thirst in a communal tomb, but that the German technicians had resisted this. We were, however, to be handed back to the SS for consignment to other camps. We wondered which.

16

The Death March

ON 5 April, 1945, when six thousand of us had already been shipped out, I saw an unknown aircraft in the sky. It was my first sight of a delta-winged plane. The huge machine passed majestically, almost silently, overhead. I guessed that it must be a German prototype being flown to safety.

More trains set off the next day. Only the Lagerkommando and the doctors and patients in the infirmary were left. The Germans burned the card indexes and other compromising documents. The camp was almost deserted now. Even the crematorium had ceased to function.

Our batch, a thousand strong, was almost the last to leave Dora. There only remained, by order of the army officer who had taken over as camp commandant, a handful of medical orderlies and prisoners pronounced too sick to travel.

Our train consisted of a dozen coal wagons and the same number of assorted carriages for the SS, who had abandoned their barracks at Nordhausen. There were also at least twenty boxcars laden with the loot they had accumulated while in occupied territory. It was a mixed bag: paintings, canteens of silver, antique furniture looted from French châteaux, even a suit of medieval armour.

The SS men were in a foul mood and treated us accordingly. Resentful that their great days were over, they took it out on those who were still at their mercy.

At long last, after many stops and detours occasioned by Allied bombs that had severed the track, we pulled into Osterode, only 45 kilometres from Nordhausen. We stopped alongside the little station's third platform. On the others glum German civilians were waiting for trains that would never turn up. It appeared that we would have to continue our journey across the Harz on foot.

The Russian prisoners in the last three

coal wagons were unloaded and marched out of the station. A minute later came the rattle of machine-gun fire, a sound which the German civilians heard with no outward emotion. Our numbers had been reduced by three hundred.

Osterode was devoid of motor vehicles capacious enough to accommodate our guards' possessions. All that remained was a motley assortment of carts. There weren't enough of them, a fact that provoked scuffles among the SS men, none of whom wanted his spoils of war left behind. In default of any horses or other draught animals to pull the overloaded carts, we prisoners were harnessed to them.

In full view of the townsfolk, we trudged through Osterode and up the winding road that led into the mountains, helped on our way by the boots, whips and rifle-butts of our guards. It was thirty-five kilometres to Goslar and the gradients *en route* ranged from one in twelve to one in seven. Exhausted men fell to their knees and were shot out of hand, to be replaced by others. From time to time a cart would go out of control on the downward slope and topple into a ravine, crushing its team of human oxen.

Our convoy proceeded on its way via Clausthal, leaving a trail of corpses in its wake. SS men who got tired of walking climbed aboard the carts and made us pull them, laughing as they urged us along with their whips like ancient Egyptian taskmasters beating slaves. It was not without reason that this nightmare trek was later called the Harz Death March.

The convoy had lost half its complement by the time we came to Goslar station, where a row of boxcars awaited us in a siding. We were permitted to lie down between the rails and enjoy a few hours' rest while the SS troopers invaded the local beer halls. Only a handful of them were left to guard us, but escape was out of the question. Their machine guns would have mown us all down.

Our numbers had dwindled to such an extent that, when we came to board the train, we did so only sixty men to a boxcar. The German organizers hadn't reckoned with such wastage, nor had they provided any latrine buckets. We had to relieve ourselves in a corner.

It proved impossible to reach our original destination, the concentration camp at Bergen-Belsen, to which other batches of prisoners had been directed. The result was that our errant train spent five days heading for each point of the compass in turn. An attempt was made to get us into Neuengamme, but the camp authorities refused to admit us or supply us with food and water. The boxcars remained closed, but we could see something of the outside world through the cracks and mesh-covered apertures in their wooden sides.

The morning of the third day came. From the position of the sun we were heading south again. '*Raus! Schnell*!' A sign on a signal box — BLOCK 7 MAGDEBURG — told us where we were. To me, who had seen the bomb damage inflicted on London, the sight of Magdeburg's charred ruins was a source of intense satisfaction, though I couldn't help wondering how many civilians had been killed by those air raids launched in the name of freedom.

344

Some fully-laden coal wagons were standing on another track. Our locomotive pulled up alongside them so that the black gold could be transferred to its tender, a task which I and a score of others were detailed to perform with our bare hands. Lumps of coal kept falling between the tracks. 'Sabotage!' yelled an SS man, and gunned down one of our number for what he deemed to be deliberate carelessness.

Another hundred prisoners had been armed with picks and shovels and ordered to dig a long trench. We wondered apprehensively if it was meant for us.

'Clean up those wagons!' yelled the SS officer who seemed to be the train commander. Gloves and pistol in hand, he strolled along the track in his high peaked cap and well-polished riding boots.

We extracted the bodies of those who had failed to survive the journey and rolled them into the trench. Then we mopped up the accumulated excrement with their clothes and tossed those in too. Finally the trench was filled in. Our lives had been spared, but why and for how much longer?

The locomotive moved on to a water tower. The train commander had an idea, a welcome one this time, probably because his nostrils were offended by the stench of our bodies in the hot April sun. Marched up to the tower, we were ordered to wash ourselves and our shit-sodden clothes in the water gushing from the canvas hose. We seized the opportunity to open our mouths and fill our bellies, heedless of the water's origin. It was like paradise after the inferno.

The train got under way again, travelling at a speed that ate up the kilometres, then came to a halt. The name on the signal box — SACHSENHAUSEN — was not unknown to us. Stationary there for many hours, we were doubtless the subject of protracted but ultimately fruitless negotiations: the camp authorities at Sachsenhausen, too, refused to take us in.

Off we went again, at first due east, then north. Strangely enough, in view of the proximity of the Russians, we seemed to be skirting Berlin.

Another day, another night. The train progressed by fits and starts, often stopping miles from anywhere. The countryside through which we were travelling was flat, sandy, and clothed in pine forests.

At last a camp hove into view, a permanent camp like Buchenwald. Here we stopped for good and were ordered out of the boxcars. Our guards marched us past the main entrance to an adjacent camp separated from the main complex by a double fence. Beyond it we glimpsed some female scarecrows who waved to us. This had to be Ravensbrück, the notorious concentration camp some 80 kilometres north of Berlin.

17

Escape from Ravensbrück

WE thought we had already plumbed the depths of human degradation, but the sights that met our eyes at Ravensbrück beggared belief. Barely recognizable as women, emaciated figures with dull, sunken eyes sank to their knees beside the barbed-wire fence and clung to it, gazing at us imploringly in the hope of seeing a friend or a dear one. Most of them were French, Belgian or Dutch. They told us that many trainloads of Poles and Czechs had left the camp in the last few days. Then they were chased away from the fence by some truncheon-wielding female SS in grey-green uniforms.

Although we had nothing with us to give the poor creatures, conditions in our own camp near the Siemens factory were positively luxurious by previous standards. There was water in plenty, and our mess-tins were amply filled with a mixture of rolled oats and lumps of meat, something we hadn't seen for months.

All became clear the next day when a Swedish Red Cross delegation visited the camp. We slept only two to a bunk, did no work and were allowed to move about freely — an unprecedented state of affairs. It was even said that future batches of prisoners would be shipped off to Sweden and interned there until the war ended, but this we strongly doubted. From what we had been told by some wagging tongues, there was a possibility we might suffer the fate of the prisoners at Neuengamme, who had been marooned aboard ships at Kiel as targets for Allied bombers.

The Swedish Red Cross had distributed food parcels, but our atrophied stomachs and intestines couldn't tolerate such a sudden influx of condensed milk, chocolate bars and corned beef. Self-restraint was difficult and the urge to gorge themselves proved fatal to some of our number.

Batches of women from the main camp departed every day, either on foot or by train. The 'Greens', who seemed to have been consigned to a separate sector, had disappeared. We spent the time strolling around, resting or chatting in small groups. The distant thunder of gunfire had been audible for the last two days and we surmised that a major battle must be in progress less than 50 kilometers south and east of us.

It was time to think about escaping, so I recruited about a dozen trustworthy friends who were eager to join me when the time came.

A few SS reappeared, accompanied by some 'Greens', most of whom now wore white armbands and carried guns. The armbands presented a problem, because my escape plan envisaged passing myself off as a 'Green', and I had already procured the requisite clothing and the triangular green patch. Some of the Red Cross parcels contained bandages, however, and these did nicely.

It was our turn to leave, this time on foot, which delighted me because it improved our chances of escape. The carts, which were drawn by horses, not, for a change, by us, were again piled high with an incredible assortment of loot, even including a child's potty-chair! Minor roads flanked by forest took us in a northwesterly direction, towards the Baltic coast. The main roads we crossed were choked with German troops retreating in disorder: One could sense that the end was near.

On some pretext one of the SS men hustled a prisoner off the road and into the undergrowth. A shot rang out, but neither man reappeared. It became clear that the trooper had donned his victim's clothes and deserted.

Our column was still too closely guarded. A prisoner ahead of us made a run for it but was promptly stopped by a bullet. I would have to be ingenious and improvise. I had promised all the members of my group who dared to take the plunge when the time came that I would lead them to the British or American lines. Transforming myself into one of the German 'Greens', a plan devised and perfected during long nights of cogitation at Dora, would not be difficult because I spoke their language.

The opportunity came at last. All the

farms we passed were deserted, their inhabitants having fled. At nightfall we were thrust into a barn and a stable filled with mooing cows. They had not been milked, so we emptied their udders for our own benefit. Afterwards, concealed behind some bales of hay, I gave my group a final briefing and metamorphosed myself into a 'Green'. The handle of a spade, which I found lying in a corner, would come in useful in the morning.

Six a.m. and '*Raus!*' The preliminary phase of the escape was about to commence. We lingered awhile to ensure that we joined the end of the column. Then, armed with my makeshift cudgel and blithely cracking them on the head with it, I hurried my friends out of the barn. The SS, who mistook me for the 'Green' in charge, suspected nothing. I had even obliterated the first digit of my number to simulate a prisoner of long standing. No German detainee would have been allotted a number in the seventy-seven thousands.

It had struck us the day before that most of the SS men escorted the carts at the front of the column while a Kubelwagen with a machine gun mounted on it brought up the rear. The remainder of the column was supervised by 'Greens'. Like them, I kept up a barrage of *Los, los, ihr Arschlöcher! Macht doch flott!*' (Make it snappy, you arseholes!) With my crew-cut and my 'smart' clothes, I looked like one of their number.

We would have to take advantage of bends in the road and the woods that flanked them to slip away without being spotted. Little by little we veered off to one side. The Kubelwagen was some three hundred metres behind. A wood, a double bend, and we were screened from view in both directions. Three of our confederates, who were unwilling to take a gamble, had positioned themselves a hundred metres ahead. They had agreed to cause a diversion by staging a scuffle as soon as I gave the prearranged signal. Our ruse succeeded: the genuine 'Greens' dashed forward to break up the fight.

Within moments we were off the road and hidden in the undergrowth. We crouched there, scarcely daring to breathe. Neither the 'Greens' nor the SS had spotted us and none of our fellow prisoners gave us away. The column continued on its way; the Kubelwagen at the rear disappeared round a bend. We were free at last.

Gauging our direction by the sun, we set off north-westwards along the forest tracks. I had effected another sartorial transformation by removing my number, the green triangle and the patches of blue-and-white striped cloth that marked me out as a concentration camp inmate. High on my left sleeve I now wore a homemade version of the Dutch military insignia, carefully fabricated during my time at Dora and hidden in my shoe since then.

Before long we heard the strains of a German marching song. We dived into the undergrowth as the voices drew nearer. To our surprise the singers started chatting among themselves in French. They were members of the *Légion Française contre le Bolchevisme*, French fascists who had talked big in the days of Germany's successes but were now, like contemptible cowards, fleeing before the Russian advance.

Our first night of freedom, a mild spring night, was spent in the forest. Although the isolated cottages we had passed looked deserted, we couldn't risk sleeping in them. Liberty was a wonderful sensation, but we were still in danger. Our close encounter with the men of the *Légion* had been an object lesson: there might be more of them around. Tomorrow would be soon enough to get organized. Meantime we settled down to sleep, revelling in the beauty of the night sky and our natural surroundings. But for the rumble of distant gunfire, we might have been Boy Scouts on a camping expedition.

In the morning we set off again. There was something eerie about the total absence of human activity. We kept one farmhouse under observation for a while but could detect no sign of life: no smoke rising from the chimney, no men at work in the fields. We decided to take a closer look.

The place was deserted, so we searched it for anything that might come in handy. We found enough civilian clothes to replace most of my companions' prison attire, but no cooking utensils or eating irons, just an old cut-throat razor. Worse still, no matches.

In a neighbouring field we came across the carcass of a white horse that must have been killed not long before, because rigor mortis had yet to set in. Using the razor, we cut ourselves some horsemeat steaks and stewed them in a mess-tin over a fire laboriously kindled with the aid of a stick, a length of string, a slab of wood and some dry moss. Water was no problem thanks to the numerous pools in the vicinity, which enabled us to quench our thirst and bathe our aching feet.

Although we had covered only twenty kilometres or so, we spent the remainder of the day resting. One of our finds at the farmhouse was an old road map, dated 1908, covering the north of Germany. Despite its antiquity, this helped us to pinpoint our position.

Next day we pressed on westwards. No more gunfire, no sign of any soldiers. Not a living soul crossed our path, not even a cat. That afternoon we came to a sizeable lake. There was a village named Vietzen near by, but we were chary of entering it. While returning to the lake to spend the night we sighted a large country house with a farm adjoining it. Although empty German ration packs in the farmyard bore witness to the passage of an army in retreat, the estate appeared to have been abandoned. It was as if an epidemic had wiped out every inhabitant. Even the agricultural machinery in the barn seemed in perfect working order. We decided to risk it. Having posted two lookouts, we installed ourselves in the farmhouse to recoup our energies for the next day's trek.

Curiosity prompted me to go and take a look at the house, which looked equally deserted. All the windows were shuttered except for one upstairs. It was open, and I thought I glimpsed a furtive figure watching me. Cautiously, I made my way around the house to the twin flights of steps that led up to the main entrance.

When I knocked the front door was opened at once by a grey-haired, well-dressed woman with aristocratic features and magnificent blue eyes. Behind her were a fair-haired girl with similar eyes and two elderly retainers. Addressing the lady of the house in German, I told her that I was a British officer who had escaped from a prison camp and was leading a party of fellow PoWs back to the Allied lines, and that all we wanted was a night's shelter. This seemed to reassure her. She said she had spotted us at the farm, which German soldiers had abandoned only that morning. Noticing that some of us were in concentration camp uniforms, she had been afraid that we would burn the place down in a spirit of revenge. When I told her that our party consisted of army officers and members of the French, Dutch and Belgian Resistance arrested by the Gestapo, she invited me into the drawing-room. The servants opened the shutters, flooding the room with evening sunlight and showing off its handsome furniture and paintings.

Instinct had prompted me to specify the Gestapo as our enemy. I realized that the woman confronting me belonged to a Junker family, and that few members of the old Prussian aristocracy had any great love for the Nazis. My instinct served me well, because I was invited to go and fetch the others. Most of them had already made themselves at home in the farmhouse and preferred to remain there with one of the servants on watch. I myself spent the night at the Schloss. The evening meal was a frugal affair. The household's stocks of food had been raided by retreating German troops, who had also denuded the estate of every last hen and rabbit, but the old maidservant produced some bottles of wine from the cellar. We drank to Germany's 'liberation' and talked until a late hour. I sensed that my hostess was happy to be able to speak freely at last, without fear of denunciation. She turned out to be a baroness and the sixteen-year-old girl was her only surviving grandchild.

The family's town house had been in Berlin, where they used to spend the winter, but it was nine years since the baroness had been there. In 1936, while she was visiting a daughter who had married in the United States, her son and daughter-in-law were arrested by the Gestapo. On returning to Germany she found that her seven-year-old granddaughter and the two old retainers had witnessed the incident. Officially her daughter-in-law had committed suicide when the secret police arrived. According to the child, they had shot her for interposing herself between them and her husband, whose fate was unknown.

For want of any alternative, the baroness had approached her brother, an ardent Nazi and senior army officer. His influence had been sufficient to preserve her from arrest, but she was banished from Berlin and the house there was confiscated. Her father was still alive at the time, so she had taken refuge with him in the country.

It was a joy to sleep in a proper bed again. Early next morning the baroness sorted through all the men's clothing she'd kept for nine years in the hope that her missing son would some day return. There were nearly a dozen pairs of shoes and boots. She was a realist. 'Your friends can have these,' she told me. 'No need to thank me, I'd sooner the Russians didn't get them.'

I left the house with a heavy heart, knowing that even harder times were in store for all who lived there. As a leaving present the baroness gave us three bicycles which had been concealed in a barn.

As we were making our way round the lake, a squadron of fighters with red stars on their wings roared low overhead. They were the first Soviet aircraft we had seen.

We were approaching Röbel. Now that we had all got rid of our prison uniforms, mingling with the mass of refugees in the village presented little danger. We learned that the Germans were still holding a line between Rostock and Rathenow. All civilians had been driven westwards into the no-man's-land between that line and the Russians, whose advance had slowed.

It was four in the afternoon when we heard the news: Hitler and Eva Braun were dead, Admiral Dönitz had taken over as head of state. There was no mention of what had happened to the other Nazi leaders. We were jubilant. It meant the end of the war, because Dönitz would undoubtedly seek an armistice.

The local inhabitants seemed stunned, especially the womenfolk, who burst into tears. For us the question was simply: Who would get here first, the Russians or the Americans? Although we naturally favoured the latter it was too late to move on that day. We found a secluded barn on the outskirts of Röbel, installed ourselves in the hay-loft and pulled up the ladder. We had the place to ourselves, or almost, because two of the Dutchmen in our party had picked up a couple of German girl refugees and were enjoying their favours. From the energetic way my compatriots performed, I could only suppose they'd consumed too much horsemeat!

Other German refugees found their way into the barn and wanted to share our snug quarters, but we fended them off. Disappointed, they bedded down on the floor.

It had been dark for several hours when we heard voices outside. The language was unintelligible, but Rozan guessed it to be Mongolian. By now shouts and screams were coming from the village. Then a woman dashed into the barn.

Breathlessly she told us that the Russians, men with Asiatic features, had entered Röbel. There weren't many of them, because the bulk of the Soviet troops were pushing south towards Pritzwalk and the Elbe so as to outflank the German forces further north.

The soldiers had found some liquor in the village. Drunk and destructive, they raped the women regardless of age. Fires broke out here and there. We had allowed the women and children among the refugees into the barn to hide in the hay with us and pulled up the ladder again. From our raised vantage-point we saw the barn door kicked open by four Russian soldiers armed with sub-machine guns. The dozen or so German menfolk, most of them elderly, were made to lie face down on the ground and systematically stripped of all their articles of value. The soldiers seemed satisfied with their booty and left without bothering to search the hay-loft. Fortunately for us, they weren't arsonists!

The sun rose on another day. For us it was a good day; for the Germans huddled in the corner of the barn, still pale with fright, it meant the end of all their grandiose ideas of *Herrenvolk* supremacy. They had been violated, not only physically but psychologically. Muttered prayers could be heard. Now that their idol was dead they were entreating the saints to preserve them.

Becoming sadistic in our turn, we took pleasure in making them fetch water for us to wash in. One of my fellow Dutchmen had told the girls we hailed from a concentration camp, and the women, fearing vengeance, offered themselves to us in return for a promise not to kill them. Happily, we retained our sense of decency and humanity.

We decided to head for the Elbe, keeping a certain distance between us and the Russian lines, in the hope of linking up with other Allied troops who would help us to get home. The village was quiet again. Most of the soldiers had moved on, but a political commissar was seated at a table in the square, scrutinizing some Germans' papers and confiscating all the money and valuables they had on them. I thought it would be useful for us to obtain a safe-conduct. Rozan explained this as best he could in the smattering of Russian he had picked up at Dora. The commissar, who was very drunk, glared at us malevolently, his eyes bleary and bloodshot with the schnapps of which he had clearly imbibed vast quantities. Papers? '*Nyet!*' A truck would come to collect us. We were German prisoners of war!

The commissar continued to eye us suspiciously. He hiccuped and belched, then vomited. Levelling his pistol, he motioned to us to clean up the mess, which stank to high heaven. Finally he heaved his fat frame out of the chair, swayed, slumped to the ground and promptly passed out. The Mongol soldiers standing nearby eyed him without compassion and motioned to us to make ourselves scarce. Our first contact with the Red Army had not been a success. We left the village as rapidly as possible.

We extricated the three bicycles from their hiding-place in the hay, but we didn't keep them for long. A road-block had been set up on the outskirts of the village. In sign language we explained that we had the commissar's permission to leave. As a form of toll we were made to surrender our new possessions. Three soldiers tried in vain to ride them, fell off, and angrily hurled them into the ditch. We observed this scene from afar but thought it wiser, having safely negotiated the check-point, not to go back and retrieve them.

At Wredenhagen the road-block was more substantial. The thoroughfare was blocked by a Russian tank of American manufacture and we were sternly forbidden to go any further. We now saw masses of armoured vehicles and well-disciplined troops advancing with the inexorability of a steamroller. That night we slept in a wood.

Up before dawn, we decided to follow the tracks of the armoured vehicles. They led south-west to a small river near Stepnitz, which in turn would surely lead us to the Elbe.

Another night in a barn. This farm had not been abandoned or devastated. The farmer's wife gave us some bread and milk, even a few eggs.

The big bridge spanning the river at

Putlitz had a check-point at one end. The Mongol soldiers manning it uttered the now traditional words '*Uhr? Uhr?*' (Watch? Watch?), but we didn't have a single timepiece between us. As partial to wrist-watches as primitive tribes to beads and baubles, the Mongols looked disappointed and demanded to see our passes. That was something else we didn't have.

Suddenly, inferring from their uncouth appearance that they couldn't read, I had an idea. Rozan and I were still in possession of the 'hair permits' that had exempted us from having our heads shorn. We produced these two documents stamped with the 'pigeon on roller-skates', as I had nicknamed the eagle and swastika, and ceremoniously handed them over. The soldier who seemed to be in charge, probably a corporal, turned them this way and that as he pretended to read them. Finally, holding them upside down, he handed them back and waved us on. *Spassiba, Russki!*

Steadfastly avoiding the main road and following the river, we got to Wittenberge. We could now see the Elbe, but all the

367

bridges were down, so we made our way along the bank in search of somewhere to cross. Although we thought we recognized some American uniforms and helmets on the other side, our waves and shouts went unanswered. We were plumb in the middle of a Russian armoured division, but the tank crews were resting and paid no attention to us. They appeared to think the war was over.

Long lines of tanks were visible in the fields across the river. We accosted one of the few Russian patrols on the bank. '*Amerikanskis?*' we asked. '*Da,*' came the reply. Aware that we would not feel truly free until we reached the other side, we spent another night in the open. We didn't look very presentable, with our stubbly chins, but that, too, could wait.

Although the bridge to Schnackenburg on the west bank had also been destroyed, men were being ferried across in rubber dinghies. Near the bridge we encountered our first Americans, who had come to greet their Russian comrades-in-arms and exchange cigarettes and candy bars for bottles of vodka. I spoke to one GI and found, not for the first time, that the world is a very small place: his home was in the Boston street where I had lived in 1938.

A Russian officer came over and addressed us in fluent English, which he spoke with a public school accent. I explained my problem. My semi-uniform must have convinced him that I was a soldier, because he told me that an agreement relating to the repatriation of prisoners had been signed at Wittenberge the day before. PoWs could cross the Elbe, but civilians had to be carefully screened, and with good reason, because it was feared that war criminals would secrete themselves among them. In short, I myself was at liberty to cross the river but my companions would have to remain behind. After much discussion, we reached a compromise. I would cross the Elbe and obtain confirmation from the Americans that my party really consisted of PoWs who had escaped from a concentration camp.

My Bostonian GI noted down their names, nationalities and numbers — if they remembered them. The only recalcitrant

members of the party were two Dutchmen, who were afraid I would leave
them in the lurch once I got across.
Their arguments were wholly negative,
like their attitude. Losing my temper, I
told them that exceptional circumstances
called for exceptional measures and that
talking big and sleeping with German girls
was a great deal easier than facing facts
and making decisions. Then I crossed the
Elbe with the GI and his friends.

At the American headquarters in
Schnackenburg I was taken to see the
lieutenant-colonel in acting command
of the local brigade. Having identified
myself as an officer in the British Secret
Service, I asked to be put in touch with
SOE and enlisted his help on behalf of
myself and my comrades, who were still
on the Russian side.

Although the colonel, a Texan, had
heard of the American OSS but never
of the SOE, he immediately radioed the
British headquarters at Salzwedel. I asked
him to help me get my party across
the river, but he said that his hands
were officially tied by the US-Soviet
agreement. I stepped up the pressure,

declaring that I would rejoin my friends unless he took some action, and that it would be his bad luck if I decided to return to the Russian side of the river now that he had transmitted my particulars to the British. I couldn't abandon the companions in misfortune who had survived death until now. More importantly, the Russians might be happy to nab some secret agents from the West.

That hit the spot. The colonel was a decent fellow at heart; it was simply that he dared not break an agreement signed by his superiors. He passed me on to a captain who, though just as insistent on observing the conventions, sent for a sergeant and briefed him. I was to go back across the river unofficially, as if on a visit, laden with cigarettes and candy bars. First, however, I was given a belated but ample breakfast of eggs and ham washed down with the most delicious real coffee.

The expedition was ready to leave. Four of us boarded a small assault craft: I myself and three Americans of whom one was the sergeant and another my GI from Boston. We would be overloaded on the return trip, if it came off, but so what, we would simply have to row a bit harder. The captain had given the sergeant his instructions: 'You're to assist this guy, but be careful, don't get caught. Just make the Russkis think it's an official operation.'

We were enthusiastically welcomed on the other side. Russian soldiers crowded round to receive their 'presents' while the members of my party, who had breakfasted with them, prepared to depart.

The English-speaking officer wasn't there any more, but it didn't matter. All that mattered was to act fast. I handed over the list of names compiled by the GI and signed by me. A Russian sergeant who had been present earlier that morning checked the numbers, which tallied, and gave the go-ahead. He was happy: he had his *papel* after all!

I lined up 'my men', gave the order and we filed down to the boat. On the way we embraced the Russian soldiers *à la russe*, happy to be seeing the last of them.

Several of us kissed the ground when we landed on the other side. Now we were truly free. GIs crowded round and showered us with presents. Our story was already the talk of the entire brigade. A welcome but unexpected surprise awaited me at headquarters, where a reply from Salzwedel had already been received: London had identified me within a couple of hours and asked that I be given every assistance.

As representatives of our respective nations, Rozan, Capelle and I shared the American officers' quarters. The others were billeted with the enlisted men, but we knew they would be in good hands.

Tomorrow arrangements would be made to get us home.

18

The Return

A SMALL Fiat army truck was placed at our disposal. It was almost new, with only 6000 kilometres on the clock, and still bore Italian military licence plates. There were no ignition keys, but that minor problem was quickly remedied by an American mechanic. As the driver, I was issued with an official movement order authorizing me to take on petrol at US and British bases and draw rations there as well.

We blithely boarded the truck and drove off, singing a musical farewell to our new-found American friends. Nine a.m. already. I stepped on the gas. It was nearly 500 kilometres to Enschede, the Dutch frontier town, and I had to stop off at Salzwedel to pick up an officer's identity card from the British headquarters there.

We experienced no problems on the

way. Driving through Hanover we got our first close-up view of a devastated German city. We had seen Magdeburg, it was true, but from a distance and with SS troopers breathing down our necks. Much of Hanover lay in ruins. We saw civilians emerge like rats from cellars and makeshift shelters. Women armed with little baskets were clearing away the rubble by hand. It was a pathetic sight, but our own recent sufferings had hardened our hearts. Minden and Osnabrück presented the same desolate appearance. We tanked up at Osnabrück and bolted a quick meal, in a hurry to leave Germany behind.

It was nine at night when we got to Enschede. We had made good time. The little truck had behaved marvellously and I felt as free as a bird.

The first soldiers we encountered were some French Canadians from the Chaudière Regiment. I asked them if there was a Dutch army barracks in the vicinity, and they told me how to get there.

At last we pulled up outside the headquarters building, where a sentry told us in bad English to get lost. I told him in his own language to pull his finger out and fetch one of his officers. An NCO appeared. He barked at me in true SS fashion. I barked even louder, threatening to charge him with insubordination towards a superior officer in the Dutch Army. He piped down at once and opened the gates. I drove in and parked the truck in the courtyard.

Next to appear, wiping his mouth, was a second lieutenant. It seemed we had interrupted his evening meal. He was in a very bad mood, and I did my best to exacerbate it. I recognized him as one of the more stuck-up members of the Princess Irene Brigade at Wolverhampton, a youngster with a university education who had chosen to go to officers' school and kill time in England, sitting on his backside, until he could return to his native land and play the conquering hero at a safe distance from the front line.

He proceeded to interrogate me as if I were a collaborator. I played along for a minute or two, then produced the military identity card issued by the British at Salzwedel, which showed that I outranked him. That took him down several pegs. He hurried to the telephone to notify his superiors. My intimate knowledge of Stratford and the Brigade had made him uneasy. I must be someone of importance, he felt, and he was scared of blotting his copybook.

The others were still outside in the courtyard, guarded by an armed sentry. As soon as I saw this I rectified the situation by emitting another series of furious barks. My companions got out and were taken to the NCOs' mess.

At last a senior officer turned up, a major whom I remembered from the Brigade and who also remembered me. He promptly fulfilled my requests. The cook was routed out of bed and told to prepare an evening meal. I myself stayed with the family on whom the major was billeted. From now on everyone went out of their way to be nice to us. Together with our host, who got out of bed and joined us, the major and I chatted far into the night. We slept little but yarned, drank and smoked a great deal.

A new day: 5 May, 1945. After a

brief night's rest I returned to the Dutch headquarters. My tongue was still thick and my insides, being unused to so much liquid refreshment, were playing up badly.

The others had been given a copious breakfast. Their tribulations of the previous night were forgotten, effaced by the warmth of their subsequent welcome. The Dutch military authorities had made a genuine effort. All the men were now equipped with underclothes, socks, blue mechanics' overalls and brand-new army boots. They had also been given a sponge-bag containing a razor and a bar of soap, a towel, and even some Dutch money. Spruced up and refreshed, I and my fellow ex-prisoners posed for a group photograph. I myself was wearing my homemade uniform, now adorned with badges of rank.

We were all itching to get home, especially my four compatriots, in spite of strong advice against continuing our journey because isolated groups of Germans were still holding out and sniping at Allied troops from concealed positions.

At my request the Fiat had been

repainted during the night and now bore distinctive marks: large white stars on the sides and orange lions on the front and rear.

A Canadian convoy was getting ready to leave for Utrecht and Amsterdam, mopping up pockets of resistance on the way. After much palaver I obtained the Canadian general's permission to join it. The Dutch authorities had provided us with permits and movement orders that would enable the Dutch among us to return home and the French and Belgians to go to Brussels. We learned that, theoretically, the Germans had laid down their arms.

The Canadian convoy, which we joined near Hengelo, made rapid progress. We drove west through Deventer to Apeldoorn, where, being the first Allied troops the townsfolk had seen, we were almost overwhelmed by cheering crowds. Here we said goodbye to the first of our party, Isaac. He was hoping to find his home intact but already knew, because he was Jewish, that he had little prospect of finding any member of his family alive. I pulled off the road and stopped. Isaac embraced me with tears in his eyes, then walked off without looking back. His joy at returning home was already clouded by the sad news that almost certainly awaited him.

The townsfolk had at first taken little notice of our truckload of civilians in blue overalls, who were almost lost among the Canadian three-tonners and armoured vehicles that were crawling through the streets, bombarded with flowers while the soldiers aboard them doled out cigarettes and candy bars.

And then a little girl with long golden hair tugged her father's hand and cried, 'Look, Papa, a Dutch lion!' She had spotted the emblem of the Netherlands Army. The father peered at me more closely, then threw up his arms and shouted, 'A Dutch officer!' The crowd surged round us. I was dragged from the driver's seat and borne along shoulder-high. Everyone wanted to touch me — to satisfy themselves that I was real. As the first Dutch officer to enter Apeldoorn on liberation day, I shall never forget that scene of unalloyed happiness or the delight on the face of that little, fair-haired girl. For the first time I truly sensed the joy that was coursing through the breasts of those who had regained their freedom after so many years. I also felt the quiet satisfaction of one who knows he has done his duty.

The convoy drove on and halted just outside Amersfoort, where we heard a few isolated shots. The original intention had been to head for Utrecht and then Rotterdam, but this was impossible because all the Rhine and Meuse bridges were down. The only way of going south was to follow a circuitous route via Zeist and Arnhem, through a no-man's-land dotted with potential ambushes.

My remaining compatriots left us, hoping to reach home under their own steam. Gerrit headed for Haarlem, Joop for Leiden and Henk for Schiedam. Impetuously eager to get home ourselves as soon as possible, we defied the advice that had been lavished on us. Where danger was concerned, we had already seen too much to be deterred.

The mopping-up operation was not complete and German soldiers were still in evidence. A comical incident occurred near Veenendaal, where two of them spotted our military vehicle and tried to surrender to us. We confiscated their weapons, pointed them in the direction of the nearest Allied troops and told them to get going. To concentration camp 'old lags' like us, disarming German soldiers was a hugely satisfying experience.

The ferry I remembered near Rhenen was out of action, so we had to drive on east regardless of the big detour this entailed. At Oosterbeek a pontoon bridge had been constructed and long columns of tanks and other military vehicles were crossing it in a northerly direction. We produced the safe-conduct requesting assistance on our behalf, but a long wait and much argument intervened before we were permitted to cross, thereby interrupting the north-bound traffic for nearly twenty minutes.

We now made rapid progress, still in the opposite direction to the troops heading north. We drove through Nijmegen and then Breda, where I intended to drop in on the Vinks. I was looking forward to a reunion with the courageous couple whom I had recruited into my network two years before, but their house was shut up and deserted. Some neighbours told me that they were alive and well but had gone away soon after the south of Holland was liberated.

Our Fiat was getting thirsty so we filled up without difficulty at a military base near the airfield at Rijen. As for us, we were getting hungry, so we stopped outside a small restaurant that looked as if it might be open. It wasn't. I explained our situation to the proprietor and produced the few florins left over from the cash we'd been given at Enschede. Not to worry, he said, and produced a regular banquet for us. Even the mayor of the little town came to make our acquaintance and we were prevailed on to recount our adventures for the umpteenth time.

The hour grew late, but we wanted to press on despite the good people's efforts to restrain us. The *patron* refused to accept a cent when we came to leave. What was more, I found a purse on the front seat of the truck containing some Belgian money to help us on our way. Our hosts had really taken us to their hearts.

It was dark by the time we drove on, but I had to pull up to allow those of our party who had eaten and drunk too much to relieve themselves by the roadside. Then Paul Capelle had an idea: he knew some people who owned a big place near Brasschaat, just short of Antwerp. Midnight had come and gone when we rang the doorbell and the master of the house appeared in a long white nightshirt that made him look like a ghost in the moonlight. After a moment's hesitation he recognized Paul and embraced him heartily. So dog-tired that we weren't even introduced to our host, we trooped inside, made a bee-line for the sofa and armchairs in the drawing-room and fell asleep without more ado. It had been a long day.

I didn't resume my place at the wheel of the Fiat until late the next morning. Paul, in company with a fellow Belgian named Hans Iwens, elected to stay on. Their families had been contacted by telephone and were coming to pick them up.

At Heist-op-den-Berg we called at the home of Lenoir the postmaster, meaning to bring his family news of him. To our absolute amazement he was there in the flesh. He had just been repatriated from Belsen, whither he had been sent from Dora with a different batch of prisoners. A man of over sixty, Lenoir had spent three years in various concentration camps, so his survival was little short of miraculous.

At Heist I put through a call to my parents in Brussels. Disguising my voice, I pretended to be a friend who had phoned to tell them that I was alive and well and would be with them in a few hours' time.

There were only three of us left when we set off for Brussels, by now only thirty-odd kilometres away. I dropped my two French friends at the Gare du Midi, where they hoped to catch a train to Paris, and covered the final stretch alone.

The horse-chestnut trees were in flower as I drove along the Avenue Louise. A minute later I was home. The door opened as I was climbing the steps. My family were waiting for me armed with bunches of my favourite lilac blossom, fresh from the garden.

19

Home at Last

IT was so good to be back, so good to sleep in my own bed once more. I toured the garden and found everything in flower: lilac trees, roses, the big weigela. The weather was warm and our horse-chestnut cast a welcome pool of shade. In a few days' time, incredible as it seemed, it would be five years since I had left home.

I noticed certain changes, for instance in the music-room. There was a space where my father's beloved grand piano used to stand. That had been bartered for food and coal-dust. My parents had needed food and warmth to survive, and money was tight because my father had a Dutch pension and no income in Belgium. The servants had all been discharged, though a faithful old cleaning-woman helped out from time to time. When it came to telling my story I hardly knew where to begin, so I described the previous five years in broad outline and filled in the details as the days went by. My parents' last, indirect word from me was two years' old, though an officer had brought them some devastating news after the liberation of Brussels the previous September: news of my arrest had reached London. I was listed as missing, presumed killed, and they had thought me safe across the Channel in England, little knowing that I had been within a few minutes of them at the end of 1943 and the beginning of 1944!

They had aged a great deal, which was hardly surprising, what with the hard times my sister and her family had been having in Austria, my brother's detention as a hostage in Holland and my own presumed death. They were overjoyed to see me again, but alarmed by my physical condition. I weighed only six stone instead of my usual ten.

I awoke late on my first morning at home. Church bells were ringing and sirens sounding a continuous 'all clear'. It was 8 May, 1945, and the war in Europe had ended. Interspersed with the Belgian national anthem, the glad tidings were broadcast again and again: the Germans had signed an instrument of unconditional surrender at Reims.

The next day I decided that, as an SOE officer, it was my duty to go and see the military attaché at the British embassy. After all, London had known of my survival for five days, ever since the word was passed to Salzwedel. I still remembered the SOE's secret 'Welbeck' phone number. General Gubbins and Major Humphries were both out when I got through, but the General's secretary inquired after my health and wondered if I could be in London in ten days' time. I said yes, and was told that the military attaché would organize a travel permit and transport. He would even come to pick me up at my home.

Meanwhile, my father had mobilized some colleagues in the medical profession who subjected me to five days of clinical tests. If they were to be believed, I was coffin meat. Lungs, stomach, intestines, joints, bones, teeth, sight, hearing — all were pronounced in very poor shape. However, I had no desire to submit to their regimens or swallow their pills. If I had survived the camps, I told myself, I could regain my health unaided as long as I didn't overdo things. My father shrewdly agreed that good morale and a determination to get well are the most effective remedies of all, and that vegetating in bed can be fatal. He was not only a qualified psychiatrist but fully aware how pig-headed I could be!

I spent my birthday, 17 May, at home. It was a quiet celebration but no less pleasant for that. Some good news reached us the same day. My brother had been released and his family were safe and well, as were my sister and her Austrian family, who had also been liberated.

I put on weight within a few days, but my new layer of fat became oedematous and required treatment.

London, May 1945

The staff car that came to collect me was very punctual, unlike me. I had been wallowing for several days in a kind of stupor, a reaction to the strain of the recent weeks that now seemed a distant memory. Fortunately my papers were in order and my suitcase had been packed since the night before, but I still had to shave and get dressed. The driver grew impatient and twice came to see if I was ready, pointing out that the plane wouldn't wait for me. I showed him the quickest way to Evere military airfield, avoiding the city centre, and he drove me there on two wheels. The Dakota was just about to take off.

I got a surprise when we landed at Croydon: General Gubbins was waiting at the foot of the gangway to welcome me in person. 'Well, young man, we thought we'd never see you again. Proud of what you achieved and happy to see you here.'

He regretted that prior commitments precluded his accompanying me back to London and entrusted me to the care of a delightful FANY, who would take me to my hotel. At Immigration I produced my travel permit and a brand-new passport issued by the Dutch consulate in Brussels, but British officials can be obstinate at times. My foreign passport was all that interested them. I was bombarded with questions. What was the purpose of my visit? Why was I in uniform when I possessed no military identity card specifying my rank? My case needed looking into. Meantime, I would have to wait.

I was escorted to an office by a constable who remained on guard at the door. The FANY, her pretty face flushed with anger at 'these desk warriors', called them 'nincompoops' and 'stupid sods' — hardly the kind of epithets one expected to hear from the lips of a well-brought-up girl. She had to wait with me while the immigration officer busied himself on the phone.

At last a more senior official, presumably his boss, appeared. He was profuse in his apologies and asked if we'd like some tea, but we told him were he could put it, cup and all. Anxious to smooth things over, he escorted us through customs without the usual inspection. He even waxed obsequious, opening the door of our waiting car and begging us to excuse 'such a regrettable error'.

The hotel was the one I had stayed at two years earlier. Before leaving me to my own devices the FANY handed me an envelope. It contained a hundred pounds, more than enough for a night on the town in congenial company, but my charming guide and protector had already disappeared. A slip of paper in the envelope requested me to present myself at Baker Street at ten the next morning.

I had the whole of the rest of the day to myself, so I seized the opportunity to reimmerse myself in the London atmosphere and make some essential purchases at the smartest military outfitters in the West End. I bought a service dress plus all the trimmings: shirt, tie, socks, shoes, commando beret, captain's pips, swagger stick, and all the insignia I was entitled to wear. The only resulting problem: remembering to return salutes in the street. Feeling almost as good as new, I spent an enjoyable few hours in a West End nightclub.

What Now?

At Baker Street, now that my mission
was at an end, I underwent prolonged
debriefing. To refresh my memory I
was shown all my network's radio
traffic. I found that my exercises in
effacing facts and superimposing fictional
incidents had been almost too successful.
Reconstructing everything in my head was
an arduous process. I flopped on my bed
that night, utterly exhausted. It took me
almost a week to edit the 92 pages and
diagrams in my report.

General Gubbins and Major Humphries
read the fruit of my labours. When next I
met the General by invitation at his club,
he introduced me as his special guest of
the day and declared that none of his
agents had ever produced as concise or
accurate a report. Winston Churchill, who
happened to be present, congratulated
me. This testimonial not only filled me
with pride but influenced the decision I
took concerning my immediate future.

My first post-war assignment was
scheduled to take me to Paris, which
had submitted a request for medals and

decorations on behalf of members of the Resistance. Some of the names on the list covering my network were wholly unfamiliar to me. Reluctant to become officially involved in this jiggery-pokery, the British authorities asked me to go to Paris and clear up the mess. However, my departure was delayed by an unforeseen circumstance.

One night after dinner I felt terribly faint and was seized with violent stomach cramps. Uncertain whether I was over-tired or merely overcome by one glass of brandy too many, I staggered to the bathroom where I vomited blood and passed out.

I regained consciousness in hospital, to be informed that I was suffering from perforated stomach ulcers. The doctor assured my friends that I would survive but prescribed a fortnight's complete bed-rest. After that, although I could barely stand, I was allowed to go home.

I spent two months on a strict diet before an X-ray confirmed that the ulcers had healed. My oedema had also dispersed. The doctors were surprised that I had recovered so quickly, but . . . no more cigarettes, no alcohol, lots of insipid baby food and plenty of rest.

I grew bored, couldn't concentrate on the books I was reading, began to be haunted by harrowing nightmares of life in captivity. I needed a change, needed to become active again and sensed that my mental equilibrium depended on it. In defiance of medical advice, I requested London for permission to go to Paris and carry out my investigation. My father was the only member of my immediate circle to approve of my going back into harness. He appreciated how much I needed activity as an aid to recuperation.

I paid a preliminary visit to London to meet the heads of SOE's French Section, who made me as welcome as a wasp at a picnic. Absolute anarchy reigned. The whole department was divided into rival factions, each of them obsessed with a single idea, namely to assert its claim to be the true saviour of France. It was very disappointing to find that unity in the face of the enemy had given way to dissension born of vested interests.

An analogous situation prevailed in Paris, except among the military, who had preserved their common sense. The man in charge of winding up my network was evasive when I asked him for the list of members he had recommended for awards, but I discovered that the original had been deposited at the Caserne de la Pépinière. On going there to examine it, I was staggered to find that it included people I'd never heard of. Completely thrown by this, I consulted my friends Émile Bollaert and General Pierre Dejussieu, 'Poncaral' in the Resistance, who had resumed his duties at Army HQ.

Pierre had no authority to intervene. Only I, as head of the network and a foreigner proof against political pressure, could set things straight. I boldly blue-pencilled some unknowns — last-minute *résistants* who had wormed their way into the ranks of the genuinely meritorious — and added two names that had been deliberately omitted.

I had the corrected list typed out and signed it the following day. This act, performed in the interests of justice, earned me the hostility of quite a few people.

That completed my final mission for SOE. Back in London once more, I was asked by General van Oorschot, who headed SOE's Dutch Section (the *Bureau Bijzondere Opdrachten*, or BBO), to go to Utrecht. Between 1942 and 1943 no less than fifty-six agents dispatched to Holland by London had fallen into enemy hands, and many matters relating to their capture required investigation. I was also to conduct a search for war criminals and interrogate them.

And that was why, after leaving Hereford House in Park Street, London, I caught a plane to Eindhoven.

20

Mission to Holland

THE BBO's Utrecht headquarters occupied a large town house belonging to Terpstra, the Dutch Laval. Operations there were directed by Major Kas de Graaf, assistant to General van Oorschot and a long-standing member of the Resistance who had escaped to England in 1944.

Of the BBO personnel I already knew, some were commandos who had been landed by parachute behind the German lines in the closing stages of the war to organize Resistance combat groups. One of these was the husband of Mies Celosse, the secretary assigned to me. Unfortunately the organization to which he had belonged before going to England had been infiltrated by Dutch agents of the SD. When he returned to Holland and renewed contact with his old network he was arrested and shot.

My original offices soon became too cramped, so I and my investigative team moved into another large house previously owned by Anton Mussert, the leading collaborator who had headed the NSB, or Dutch National Socialist Movement. Holland's status as an occupied country differed from that of France and Belgium. It had been annexed and was governed by the former gauleiter of Austria, 'Reich Commissioner' Arthur Seyss-Inquart, with Mussert's assistance.

A few days after my arrival in Holland I went to see my brother, who lived near The Hague. I had the greatest respect for him and his wife, whose courageous attitude during the occupation had been exemplary. Managing director of the local subsidiaries of a French-owned group, the Compagnie Générale d'Électricité, my brother had been taken hostage by the Germans. Luck was with him, however, because he escaped the fate of some other prominent citizens. His brother-in-law and four of his friends had been lost at sea while trying to reach England in an open boat.

Now I could get down to work. Several

senior SD officers such as Haubrok and Schreieder were in Dutch prisons. It was my job to question them, winkle out the collaborators who had helped them, and reconstruct the details of the '*Nordpolspiel*' or '*Englandspiel*', the Germans' greatest counter-espionage coups against the Dutch Resistance.

Although my team's investigations led to the arrest of many culpable traitors and war criminals, I was deeply disgusted by the fact that, as Allied interrogators, we had to work alongside a devil's advocate of a lawyer who lacked any conception of the Germans' own interrogation methods, let alone the predicament in which members of the Resistance had found themselves. He forbade us to submit personal conclusions based on fact unless we had obtained a confession, duly signed by the perpetrator of a criminal act, that acknowledged his guilt or complicity.

It was clear that the perverted brutes responsible were making fun of us. Remembering the treatment I myself had received at their colleagues' hands, I would happily have given them a dose of their own medicine, but it was not to be. As a result, many genuine war criminals were released for want of tangible evidence and are still living overseas, often in luxury — and this although the 'Nordpolspiel' cost the lives of the fifty-six parachute agents and their associates.

To clear up certain doubts concerning the possibility of treason, I went to London to examine the originals of the radio messages exchanged during 1942 and 1943 by the Dutch Resistance and the Dutch Section of SOE.

If arrested, wireless operators were entitled to save their lives by continuing to transmit under enemy control. In such cases, however, they had to change the letters of their security code so that London would know they were in enemy hands and transmitting messages concocted by the Germans.

I found, alas, that it was human to err. Messages were often garbled during transmission, and the decoders in London, knowing where the actual text began, had developed a regrettable and all too frequent habit of ignoring the groups of letters that made up the security code. What contributed to this habit was that the young women who monitored the messages became so good at recognizing a particular wireless operator's 'fist' that they took his or her transmissions on trust. The transcript of a deciphered message was supposed to be forwarded to the relevant national section bearing a note certifying that the security code had been checked. Unfortunately, this note was often omitted. Bred by routine, this second sin of omission had very grave consequences.

The '*Nordpolspiel*', a brilliant scheme devised by an NCO in German radio intelligence, had its origin in the relatively commonplace arrest of a wireless operator named Hubertus Lauwers, whom the Abwehr had imprisoned at Scheveningen. The NCO submitted the idea to his superior officer, Major Hermann Giskes, head of the Abwehr in Holland, and Giskes decided to act on it.

The network to which Lauwers belonged had been penetrated by a German agent named Ridderhof, who passed some genuine and important information to Taconis, his head of network. When this text, duly enciphered by Taconis, was transmitted to London, the Germans intercepted it. Giskes, who had drafted the text himself, was thus in possession of the wording both in code and in clear. It was child's play, therefore, for German cryptographers to find the key to the code. Taconis was also arrested but imprisoned separately from his wireless operator.

When, under duress, Lauwers agreed to transmit for the Germans from prison, he not only garbled his security code but on one occasion actually transmitted the word 'caught' in clear. Even that message, which I saw with my own eyes, failed to ring any alarm bells in London!

The outcome of these transmissions, drafted by Giskes in Taconis's code, was catastrophic. Mingling fact with fiction, the Abwehr succeeded in convincing the Dutch Section in London that all was well — that the network was expanding its activities, and that more organizers and wireless operators should be dispatched to enhance its effectiveness.

That was how fifty-odd brave men left England, never to return, and fell straight into the hands of the Germans. Since they were strangers to the networks they were supposed to contact, it was easy enough to replace them with Dutchmen working for the Germans and penetrate the heart of the Dutch Resistance.

The double game only ended when the two agents, Dourlein and Ubbink, whose escape is mentioned in Chapter 12, contrived to flee from Haren prison in Holland and reach safety in Switzerland. There, at London's request, I managed to establish their *bona fides*. Lauwers was deported to Germany but survived. Our inquiries cleared him of all suspicion.

The unification of the Dutch Resistance movements, a policy advocated early in 1943, came to nothing. Responsibility for this rested equally with the British and the Dutch themselves, who had caused the above catastrophe by failing to observe certain strict and indispensable rules. The heads of the Dutch Section were sacked and replaced by a new organization, the *Bureau Bijzondere Opdrachten* to which reference has already been made. General van Oorschot and Kas de Graaf, who had recently come from Holland, were fully acquainted with local conditions from both the Resistance and the German point of view. It was under their leadership that another hundred-odd agents were parachuted into Holland and carried out successful missions there in the closing months of the war.

Not for the first time, my interrogation of Germans and their collaborators demonstrated the essential spinelessness of many members of the human race, a quality that distressed me every time I encountered it. My 'subjects' were not major war criminals but men who had one day, through fear or self-interest, inserted their finger in the pie and compromised themselves by entering the invader's service. I rejected many offers that would have set me up for life from those who, having been corrupted themselves, hoped to regain their freedom by corrupting someone else. I was almost equally disgusted by the in-fighting and incomprehension of the lawyers and judges assigned to review their cases. It made me wonder why so many brave men had sacrificed their lives.

Thoroughly disillusioned, I requested permission to take a long spell of demobilization leave in the South of France. One chapter of my life had ended; another was about to begin.

21

At Peace in Provence

C IVILIAN life had reclaimed me. It was April, the season when Provence lavishes all its treasures on those fortunate enough to be there at that time of year: sunshine, blue skies, luxuriant flowers and blossom — all the things that betoken Nature's cycle of rebirth.

I was reunited with the friends who, from my earliest childhood, had constituted my second family. Jacqueline, the girl whom I used to regard as a little sister, had become a young woman, matured by her contacts with the Resistance. A member of the Red Cross, she had volunteered for a number of dangerous assignments, likewise for service in a team that identified dead bodies retrieved from the ruins of bomb-damaged buildings. Thanks to the heat of the southern sun and the time it took to extricate them, many such corpses were in a state of advanced decay. It was a long time before Jacqueline could endure the sight of spaghetti; she had seen too many maggots proliferating in the intestines of the dead.

Her grandparents' house in the hills above Aix was an oasis of tranquillity and it was there that I at last found the repose I needed so badly. My mind had been affected even more than my body. Utterly disoriented, I suffered from mood swings and fits of irritability that called for superhuman feats of patience on the part of my friends. Jacqueline's parents, who had the gift of understanding, looked on me as a son. Better still, Jacqueline agreed to become my wife.

Epilogue

ALMOST fifty years have gone by and I'm sitting on the terrace of the same old house in the hills above Aix. The peace and quiet would be absolute but for the sound of the water-laden Canadair tankers and other fire-fighting aircraft that regularly fly past. For several days now, my family and I have been watching smoke and flames engulf huge tracts of the lovely Provençal countryside so dear to Cézanne. These forest fires conjure up scenes so reminiscent of the horrors of war that my dreams have been haunted by nightmare visions from the past. Half a century has done nothing to dull their intensity.

I feel no hatred, just a kind of lassitude mingled with resentment of the human folly so often provoked by ideology and self-interest — resentment of people's failure to recognize the duty they owe their neighbours, the golden rule without which life becomes a hell on earth. Freedom of thought is the inalienable right of every man and woman, but the right to assert oneself must not encroach on others or do them harm.

Our grandchildren are spending the summer holidays with us. It was for them, the youngest members of our family, that I finally decided to write this book. I wanted it to be not only a dispassionate record of events but instructive and, where possible, relieved by the sense of humour that is one of our most effective aids to survival. I wanted it to show how, even in the depths of adversity and despair, an ideal can illumine our darkness like a guiding star. By its clear light we can enjoy such moments of happiness as come our way, sometimes in the most unexpected guises.

Living in peace is harder than making war, because it calls for concessions freely made and a willingness to sympathize with the concerns of others. Times may have changed in the age of computers and space travel, but the fundamental problems remain. It behoves those of my advanced years to establish a rapport with the younger generation and impart such lessons as we have learned in a language they can understand.

Creatures of the wild often display a more unerring instinct than human beings. Yesterday, put to flight by the smoke and flames, a little bird sought refuge on our terrace. Hungry and thirsty, exhausted and dishevelled, it perched on my wife's shoulder and instantly went to sleep. Thereafter it accompanied her everywhere, riding on her shoulder even when she went indoors to prepare a meal. It is still with us this morning, cheerfully treating us to a recital of chirps and trills from the trees overhead or perching on my shoulder and gently pecking my ear as I write. In its panic and confusion, it sought out friends in need. Such friends are always to be found. We have only to look for them and, in so far as we are able, to repay them in kind. By singing and keeping me company, that little bird has more than repaid me: it has warmed my heart.

Living in peace entails complying with the rules that should govern communal

412

life in any society. Transgressing those rules is always a crime against humanity. It is only the common good that entitles us to take ruthless action, cross swords with an aggressor and nip an evil in the bud. Any dragon that threatens to devour us and our dear ones must be slain without compunction. When plague is spreading rats are fair game. That was the sentiment which sustained me throughout the Second World War.

'Why exist at all?' ask the more cynical and less idealistic members of the younger generation. They need only look around them, and it is up to us, who have learned so much from bitter experience, to open their eyes.

The key to happiness? A perception of the beauties our world has to offer, from the little flowers that thrust their heads above the winter snow, heralding a new spring, to the love that shines in the eyes of men, women and children bound by the family ties that continue to form the basis of our society, even in an age when such bonds are too often severed.

An appreciation of simple joys and the determination to preserve them intact — that should be our guiding light. May it lead the human race, step by step, toward its ultimate goal: a world at peace.

GUIDO Z. SCHREVE
alias PIERRE LALANDE

Aix-en-Provence, August 1989

Other titles in the
Ulverscroft Large Print Series:

TO FIGHT THE WILD
Rod Ansell and Rachel Percy

Lost in uncharted Australian bush, Rod Ansell survived by hunting and trapping wild animals, improvising shelter and using all the bushman's skills he knew.

COROMANDEL
Pat Barr

India in the 1830s is a hot, uncomfortable place, where the East India Company still rules. Amelia and her new husband find themselves caught up in the animosities which seethe between the old order and the new.

THE SMALL PARTY
Lillian Beckwith

A frightening journey to safety begins for Ruth and her small party as their island is caught up in the dangers of armed insurrection.

THE WILDERNESS WALK
Sheila Bishop

Stifling unpleasant memories of a misbegotten romance in Cleave with Lord Francis Aubrey, Lavinia goes on holiday there with her sister. The two women are thrust into a romantic intrigue involving none other than Lord Francis.

THE RELUCTANT GUEST
Rosalind Brett

Ann Calvert went to spend a month on a South African farm with Theo Borland and his sister. They both proved to be different from her first idea of them, and there was Storr Peterson — the most disturbing man she had ever met.

ONE ENCHANTED SUMMER
Anne Tedlock Brooks

A tale of mystery and romance and a girl who found both during one enchanted summer.

CLOUD OVER MALVERTON
Nancy Buckingham

Dulcie soon realises that something is seriously wrong at Malverton, and when violence strikes she is horrified to find herself under suspicion of murder.

AFTER THOUGHTS
Max Bygraves

The Cockney entertainer tells stories of his East End childhood, of his RAF days, and his post-war showbusiness successes and friendships with fellow comedians.

MOONLIGHT
AND MARCH ROSES
D. Y. Cameron

Lynn's search to trace a missing girl takes her to Spain, where she meets Clive Hendon. While untangling the situation, she untangles her emotions and decides on her own future.

NURSE ALICE IN LOVE
Theresa Charles

Accepting the post of nurse to little Fernie Sherrod, Alice Everton could not guess at the romance, suspense and danger which lay ahead at the Sherrod's isolated estate.

POIROT INVESTIGATES
Agatha Christie

Two things bind these eleven stories together — the brilliance and uncanny skill of the diminutive Belgian detective, and the stupidity of his Watson-like partner, Captain Hastings.

LET LOOSE THE TIGERS
Josephine Cox

Queenie promised to find the long-lost son of the frail, elderly murderess, Hannah Jason. But her enquiries threatened to unlock the cage where crucial secrets had long been held captive.

THE TWILIGHT MAN
Frank Gruber

Jim Rand lives alone in the California desert awaiting death. Into his hermit existence comes a teenage girl who blows both his past and his brief future wide open.

DOG IN THE DARK
Gerald Hammond

Jim Cunningham breeds and trains gun dogs, and his antagonism towards the devotees of show spaniels earns him many enemies. So when one of them is found murdered, the police are on his doorstep within hours.

THE RED KNIGHT
Geoffrey Moxon

When he finds himself a pawn on the chessboard of international espionage with his family in constant danger, Guy Trent becomes embroiled in moves and countermoves which may mean life or death for Western scientists.

TIGER TIGER
Frank Ryan

A young man involved in drugs is found murdered. This is the first event which will draw Detective Inspector Sandy Woodings into a whirlpool of murder and deceit.

CAROLINE MINUSCULE
Andrew Taylor

Caroline Minuscule, a medieval script, is the first clue to the whereabouts of a cache of diamonds. The search becomes a deadly kind of fairy story in which several murders have an other-worldly quality.

LONG CHAIN OF DEATH
Sarah Wolf

During the Second World War four American teenagers from the same town join the Army together. Forty-two years later, the son of one of the soldiers realises that someone is systematically wiping out the families of the four men.